Economics Terms

John Samuel Dodds

Chambers Commercial Reference

© W & R Chambers Ltd Edinburgh, 1987

Published by W & R Chambers Ltd Edinburgh, 1987

All rights reserved. No part of this publication may be reproduced or transmitted in any form or by any means, electronic or mechanical, including photocopying, recording or any information storage or retrieval system, without prior permission, in writing, from the publisher.

We have made every effort to mark as such all words which we believe to be trademarks. We should also like to make it clear that the presence of a word in this book, whether marked or unmarked, in no way affects its legal status as a trademark.

British Library Cataloguing in Publication Data
Dodds, J. S.
    Economics.—(Chambers commercial reference)
    1. Economics—Dictionaries
    I. Title
    330'.03'21   HB61
ISBN 0-550-18064-8

Typeset by Blackwood Pillans & Wilson Ltd Edinburgh
Printed by Richard Clay Ltd, Bungay, Suffolk

Preface

Economics Terms is a compact but comprehensive reference book which has been specially written to meet the needs of school and college students on a wide range of business and vocational courses at intermediate level.

Along with the other titles in the Chambers Commercial Reference series, *Economics Terms* provides up-to-date explanations of the key terms used in various areas of business activity. All words and abbreviations are listed alphabetically and defined in clear, simple English.

Although intended as a companion to course studies, *Economics Terms* is also an ideal reference text for those already working in a commercial environment. The book will prove to be an invaluable companion to their work.

Other titles in this series

Bookkeeping and Accounting Terms
Business Terms
Office Practice Terms
Office Technology Terms

Economics Terms
John Samuel Dodds was former Assistant Secretary (Examinations) with the North Western Regional Advisory Council for Further Education. His work centred on the design, revision and publication of syllabuses and examination schemes, particularly in business subjects.

Aa

abnormal profit   The excess of actual profit over normal profit. It is the income that rewards the owner's enterprise in setting up the firm and taking the business risks. If entry into a particular business activity is perfectly free, then in the long run abnormal profits will reduce to zero. This is due to the competition of new entrepreneurs attracted to the market by the prospect of higher incomes than they are currently earning. Thus abnormal profit is either a short-run disequilibrium phenomenon or the result of barriers to entry. Also known as **supernormal profit.**

above the line transactions   Items in the balance of payments accounts which record total payments and receipts on visible and invisible trade and on investment and capital transactions.

absolute cost advantage   The advantage possessed by a country when with a given quantity of productive resources it can produce more of a particular commodity than other countries. Also the advantage of existing firms who, owing to their established control of supply and production techniques, enjoy lower average costs than new incoming firms.

absolute monopoly   A theoretical market structure used in economic analysis which assumes the existence of all the characteristics of monopoly in their most pure form.

abstinence   Restricting the manufacture of consumer goods so that the productive resources so released may be switched to increasing the stock of capital goods. The resulting expanded manufacturing capacity will in the future enable a greater output of consumer goods than at present.

accelerating inflation   An inflation whose rate of increase rises continuously.

acceleration principle

acceleration principle The relationship between a sustained rise in the sales of a commodity and the increase in the ordering by firms of the extra factory equipment made necessary by the increased output. With unchanged demand, the firms' orders for factory equipment are at a relatively low level which is just sufficient to meet replacement requirements. A sustained rise in output involves the firm in raising its productive capacity and installing extra factory equipment in addition to replacement needs. This could double, treble or quadruple the orders for capital equipment.

accelerator coefficient The figure by which a given percentage rise in a firm's output must be multiplied in order to find the percentage increase in the level of ordering by a firm of factory equipment to provide itself with the extra productive capacity necessary to meet the rise in output.

action lag The time that elapses between a decision to take a particular course of action and the action itself.

ad valorem tax A tax levied on goods 'according to (their) value'. It is calculated by multiplying the value of the goods by the agreed percentage of the tax.

adverse balance of payments One which is in deficit, that is, total annual payments to other countries exceed total receipts from other countries.

adverse balance of trade The situation when the value of a country's imports exceeds the value of its exports.

agents of production Factors of production.

aggregate demand Aggregate expenditure.

aggregate expenditure The total spending of all buyers of capital and consumer goods and services produced in a country. This includes the spending of households, firms, local and central government, together with income from exports less imports.

aggregate price levels An index number which concentrates into a single figure the price levels of a range of selected goods or services by relating them to their price levels at some given base date.

assumptions

aggregate supply A country's total output of capital and consumer goods and services in response to aggregate expenditure. It consists of home-produced goods and services plus imports.

allocation of resources The determination of the uses to which productive resources will be put. Resources are scarce relative to the total flow of goods and services that society would like to produce with them. This scarcity creates the need for allocation.

applied economics That branch of economics which applies the hypotheses and analytical techniques of theoretical economics to the consideration of practical problems.

appreciation A rise in the value of an asset. It may be due to inflationary price rises, the increasing scarcity of the asset in relation to demand, or a general rise in purchasing power.

articles of ostentation Goods whose appeal to some people is that they are obviously, or are well known to be, expensive. Since their expense is an essential part of the attraction of such goods, a rise in their price may result in more being bought.

assets Everything that an individual or a firm owns which has a money value. A distinction is made between 'real' or 'tangible' assets such as land, buildings or machinery, and 'financial' assets such as cash holdings, bank deposits, securities, the amounts owed by debtors or the value of goodwill and patents.

assumptions The economic world is extremely complex with many causes and effects interacting at the same time. If we wish to study the effect of one particular cause on one particular aspect of the economic system (for example, the effect on a product's output of the imposition of a price control) then we can identify certain factors (the market forces affecting supply and demand) that are essential to the analysis. There are also many other factors, such as the reaction of exporters or overseas suppliers of the product or its raw materials, which in reality would influence the situation. To attempt to include these would, however, cloud the main issues on which we wish to concentrate. To avoid such confusion it is necessary to simplify the problem by making a preliminary set of 'assumptions' about the behaviour of these background influences, or simply to assume a closed economy and hence their non-existence.

autarky The situation of a country which is a closed economy conducting no international trade.

automatic stabilisers Compensatory mechanisms within the economy that modify inflationary or deflationary fluctuations. They are immediately self-initiating and avoid the time lags that otherwise would be required for individual central policy decisions. For example, the reduction in aggregate demand due to rising unemployment is relieved to the extent that the unemployed receive benefits and are not forced to cut their spending as much as they would otherwise. Alternatively, a rise in aggregate demand caused by an inflationary wage spiral is modified by the reductions in disposable income arising from a progressive income tax.

average cost pricing A method of fixing the price of a good by adding a gross profit margin on to its average variable costs so as to cover its average total cost of production. This markup comprises an overhead element and a fixed net profit margin regarded as normal for the industry.

average fixed cost Fixed costs divided by the number of units of output. With an increasing output, the unchanging fixed costs are spread more widely over an increasing number of units so that average fixed costs decline.

average income A statistic for a particular sub-division of the population such as 'households'. It is found by dividing the national income by the number of units in the group.

average productivity of labour An indicator of productive efficiency used for purposes of comparison over time or between industries. It is found by dividing output by numbers employed or by man-hours worked.

average propensity to consume The proportion of an individual's disposable income or a country's national income spent on consumer goods and services. It is found by dividing the consumption spending by the income.

average propensity to save The proportion of an individual's disposable income or a country's national income not spent on consumer goods and services, that is, which is saved. It is found by dividing the saving by the income.

average rate of return on capital Net profit as a percentage of average capital employed in a business. One of a number of financial ratios used to measure the efficiency of a business or a particular investment project.

average revenue An alternative way of stating 'price'. The total revenue received from the sale of a given number of units of output, divided by that number of units.

average tax rate For the country this is the percentage of the national income that is paid in tax. For an individual it is the percentage of his income before tax that he pays in tax.

average total cost The total of the fixed and variable costs of producing a given number of units of output divided by that number of units.

average variable costs The total variable costs of producing a given output divided by the number of units of that output.

avoidable costs Costs which arise exclusively from the production process and which would not be incurred if no output took place. They are to be distinguished from fixed costs which would still have to be met at zero output. They are mostly variable costs incurred directly in producing the output but additionally include other indirect costs such as a proportion of the salaries of clerical and administrative staff.

Bb

backward bending labour supply curve A graphical presentation of the situation where an increase in wage rates results in fewer man-hours being worked. When the wage rate rises the worker experiences two opposing effects. As each extra working hour is more valuable, there is an incentive to work longer hours. But there is also a disincentive because extra income can now be earned with fewer hours, making it possible both to have more leisure and more money to spend. Beyond a certain point, the increasing unpleasantness of each extra hour worked and the increasing sense of loss at each hour of leisure sacrificed, causes the disincentive effect to begin to outweigh the incentive effect of earning more money, and the worker will prefer to work fewer hours.

backward bending supply curve A regressive supply curve.

backward integration The action of a firm which extends its range of activities to take in contributory stages of production. A retail organisation may establish or acquire a wholesaling organisation to feed its outlets, or may extend further into the manufacturing stages of the products in which it is involved.

balance for official financing In the balance of payments account this records how the overall deficit or surplus of the current and capital accounts has been financed by transfers into and out of the country's reserves of gold and foreign currencies or by borrowing from other governments.

balance of payments A tabulation summarising a country's payments to the rest of the world over a month, quarter or year, and its receipts from other countries. These transactions are presented under the three headings of *current account, capital account* and *official financing*. The current account is further sub-divided into *visible trade account* and *invisible trade account*.

balance of payments balancing item The balance of payments account unavoidably contains many inaccuracies and omissions. This is because of the time lag before settlement of the payments for imports and exports produces accurate information. To deal with this, a balancing item representing the net total of the errors and omissions is calculated and entered in the account.

balance of payments capital account This records the inward and outward money payments for private and official transfers of capital on investments, international grants and loans and other forms of government overseas expenditure. The account has a deficit balance when a country's total payments to foreign countries exceeds its receipts from them, and a surplus in the reverse situation.

balance of payments current account This records the balances for visible trade and invisible trade. It shows the relation between the total amount received by supplying goods and services to other countries and the amount spent in buying goods and services from them. The net total of these balances gives a surplus when exports exceed imports, or a deficit when imports exceed exports.

balance of payments deficit The overall balance of the current and capital accounts if payments to overseas countries exceeds receipts from them.

balance of payments surplus The overall balance of the current and capital accounts if receipts from overseas countries exceeds payments to them.

balance of trade deficit The balance on visible account when the value of a country's imports is greater than that of its exports. This is described as an adverse balance of trade.

balance of trade surplus The balance on visible account when the value of a country's exports is greater than that of its imports. This is described as a favourable balance of trade.**balance of visible trade** The difference between the monetary value of all goods imported into a country and the monetary value of those it exports.

balanced budget A government budget is in balance when the estimated revenue from taxation equals the sum needed to finance its proposed expenditure.

bank credit creation When a bank lends, the borrower's account is credited with the amount of the loan. But the bank does not lose the use of a sum equal to the amount borrowed in order to make the loan. It creates what it lends. Thus bank current account deposits, which form part of the money supply, rise by this amount and total purchasing power increases.

bank current account balances Bank deposits which are withdrawable or transferable by cheque without notice. They form part of the money supply.

Bank of England The publicly-owned central bank of the United Kingdom that acts as link between the Government and the country's banking system for implementing the Government's financial and monetary policy. (1) It acts as banker and financial adviser to the Government, holding the deposits of Government departments including that of the Exchequer which receives the proceeds of taxation. It manages the Government's revenues and expenditure, covering any temporary deficit by borrowing. (2) It acts as banker to the high street banks, keeping their accounts and holding their cash reserves. (3) It controls the total money supply by regulating the issue of bank notes (in England) and coins, and through the level of their cash reserves the credit policy of the banks who can extend credit to their customers only up to a certain multiple of the value of their cash reserves. (4) It manages the national debt, supervising the issue and redemption of Government loans. (5) It conducts transactions between Britain and the central banks of other countries and international financial institutions such as the International Monetary Fund. It administers the foreign exchange control regulations, engaging in dealings in foreign currencies so as to control the rate of foreign exchange, buying and selling gold and managing the level of sterling holdings overseas. (6) It is the 'lender of the last resort', that is, it has to guarantee the financial stability of the banking system by providing funds to prevent the insolvency of financial institutions and a possible loss of confidence in the economy.

bank reserves Only a small proportion of the value of a bank's deposits is demanded in cash (notes and coin) at any given time. Most transactions take place by cheque or credit transfer. A bank must, however, always be prepared to pay cash on demand. For this purpose, it maintains a cash reserve of a definite ratio, the *cash ratio*, to its deposits.

barriers to entry Factors that place potential new entrants to an industry at a disadvantage relative to established firms. These can take a number of forms. Existing firms may own essential raw materials, technology or patent rights not available to newcomers. They may be protected from competition by government regulations. As developed firms, they will enjoy economies of scale, new entrants being faced with high initial costs of establishment and a develpoment period of high average fixed costs.

barter The direct trading of goods or services for other goods or services, without using any commonly accepted medium of exchange.

base period A particular date used as a reference point on which to collect specified data so that it may be compared with corresponding data collected at successive later dates. The comparison is usually made by converting the data to an index number which starts with the value of 100 at the base date.

below the line transactions Transactions in the balance of payments accounts which show how the overall debit or credit

bilateralism

balance on the current and capital accounts above the line has been financed. They include such items as the changes in the balance of gold and foreign currency reserves or the extent of foreign loans.

bilateralism An agreement between two countries regarding the type, quantity or value of the exports of one to the other, and extending to each other advantageous trading arrangements which they do not extend to outsiders.

birth rate The average number of live births occurring in a year for every 1000 of the population.

black market An illicit trade which tends to develop in a product for which, owing to its shortage and the need to ensure its fair allocation among the people, the Government has fixed a selling price at a level within the reach of most. To avoid a 'first come first served' or customer favouritism situation, it is often also necessary to supplement the price control by rationing. The official price is thus below that which some customers would be willing to pay if it were unrestricted and able to rise to its equilibrium level. In these circumstances there are always persons who are prepared to take advantage of the difference between the controlled price and the equilibrium price and, if there is rationing, the difference between the ration allocation and the amount that customers would like to obtain. Such 'black marketeers' obtain supplies of the scarce product and resell them illegally at above the controlled price. The customer thus has two sources of supply: the 'legitimate' market selling at the controlled price (possibly against ration coupons), and the 'black' market selling at variable higher prices with no question of coupons.

boom The upper phase of the expansionary period of the trade cycle typified by increasing demand, rising sales and profits. As the phase develops it becomes increasingly difficult to raise output in response to increasing demand because the supply of unused industrial capacity and pool of unemployed workers is diminishing. Shortages start to develop in supplies of essential productive resources. Output

budget deficit financing

can be raised only through net investment for which borrowing takes place. Because of the time lag however, immediate rises in demand result in price increases rather than in increases in supply. Business remains generally profitable because cost increases can be passed on in rising prices, and expectations for the future remain optimistic.

break-even level of income That at which spending on goods and services is exactly equal to income. Above this level, spending is less than income and saving takes place. Below this level, spending is greater than income and dissaving takes place through borrowing or drawing on past savings.

break-even volume of production The minimum output required, at a given selling price, to ensure that a firm's total cost of production is covered. This output is found by dividing the fixed costs by the difference between the selling price and the variable cost per unit.

budget A financial statement by a government of its proposed current and capital spending in a future period and its estimates of how that spending will be financed by taxation revenue and by borrowing.

budget constraint A schedule listing the various combinations of two goods that a consumer can afford to buy within the limits of his income and the prices of the goods. He can spend all his income on one good and have none of the other, or can balance his spending between varying quantities of the two, more of one necessitating less of the other.

budget deficit The excess of the government's spending over its receipts from taxation.

budget deficit financing A deliberate budgeted excess of government expenditure over income. Its object is to stimulate economic activity and employment by injecting more purchasing power into the economy. The excess expenditure is financed by borrowing.

budget line The line joining the points on a graph which plot the various combinations of two goods given in a budget constraint schedule. It shows the combinations of two goods that the consumer can buy, given his income and their prevailing prices. The consumer's most satisfactory allocation of spending between the goods is the point on the budget line where an extra poundsworth of spending on either good gives him the same increase in satisfaction.

budget share The percentage of total spending on consumer goods and services allocated to a particular good or service in a given period.

budget surplus The amount by which government receipts from taxation exceed its spending.

built-in stabilisers Automatic stabilisers.

burden of indirect taxation The incidence of indirect taxation.

business cycle The trade cycle.

buyers' market A market in a situation of excess supply. Sellers cannot clear all their output at the prevailing prices and are forced to reduce prices to compete for buyers who are relatively scarce and able to obtain favourable terms.

by-product A product which is the unavoidable secondary output of a process designed primarily to produce another product.

Cc

capital One of the traditional groupings of productive resources which together with labour and land formed the three factors of production. It comprises the stock of goods, accumulated by past production, used solely to increase the productivity of labour and land in the provision of consumer goods and services and other capital goods. It consists of all types of buildings, machinery, equipment, means of communication and transport together with stocks of raw materials and unsold goods.

capital accumulation An increase in a country's stock of capital goods. This involves the diversion of productive resources from the provision of consumer goods and services not only to the replacement of worn-out or obsolete buildings and equipment, but additionally to the enlargement of the stock of such goods.

capital consumption Failure to replace worn-out capital goods used up in the process of production. This results in a diminishing stock of capital. It occurs if too great a proportion of resources are used to produce consumer goods and services, for then insufficient resources will be available for making replacement capital goods.

capital deepening The building up by a firm of a greater ratio of capital goods to manpower.

capital depreciation The wearing out of capital goods or the running down of stocks of raw materials and finished or semi-finished goods.

capital expenditure Expenditure by households, firms, the government or its agencies on replacing worn-out capital goods, or increasing the stock of them.

capital formation Capital accumulation.

capital goods Capital.

capital intensive Descriptive of that type of production process, industry or economy in which there is a high ratio of capital goods' cost to the cost of the workforce and other resources employed.

capital-labour ratio The proportion in which capital goods and manpower are combined in a particular production method.

capital-labour substitution The action by a firm in changing the proportion in which capital goods and manpower are combined in a production method.

capital-output ratio A measure to enable international comparison of the productive efficiency of a country's capital stock. The value of the capital stock is divided by the national output that it has helped to produce. This gives the average value of the capital employed per unit of output.

capital stock A country's total supply of all types of industrial and commercial buildings, machinery, equipment, means of communication and transport, together with stocks of raw materials, semi-finished goods and unsold goods.

capital widening When an expanding firm increases its capital goods and its workforce in the same proportion so that there is no change in the capital-labour ratio.

capitalism An economic system in which the land is privately owned by landlords and the commercial and industrial productive assets are privately owned by capitalists. Acting individually or collectively through firms, they employ the workers and, in response to market forces, make the decisionson the nature and quantity of the goods and services to be supplied.

captive market One where there is a sole supplier of a good or service which the customers cannot do without and for which they cannot obtain any acceptable substitute.

cash Money in the sense of coins, notes and bank current account deposits on which cheques can be drawn.

cash flow The difference between the payments received by a firm in a given period and the payments that it makes. This is the net amount of money the firm actually retains. Cash flow may be low even when profits are high if the firm has to meet costs promptly but its customers take a long time to settle their bills.

cash ratio Cash reserve ratio.

cash reserve ratio The ratio of a bank's cash holdings to its total deposit liabilities to its customers. The minimum ratio is usually fixed by law or is subject to the control of the central bank.

ceiling prices Maximum levels imposed by the government on the prices of certain goods or services.

central bank The bank which in any country is the link between the government and the banking system. It is the agency through which the government carries out its monetary policy of controlling the credit system, the interest rate, the note issue, the foreign exchange rate and the transfer of money and bullion with the central banks of other countries. It acts as the government's bank and the bankers' bank.

centrally controlled economy An economy where the government makes the decisions about production, consumption and the allocation of resources. Central planning offices decide what will be produced, how much, in what manner, and for whom, and allocate productive resources among the various producers in accordance with these decisions, so that firms and consumers produce and consume only as they are ordered. In reality such absolute conditions do not exist. How much choice firms and individuals will retain depends on the extent of the planning. Some countries exercise greater central control than others.

ceteris paribus A Latin phrase meaning 'other things being equal'. Used in economics to indicate in an argument that while certain values are to be altered, others are presumed to remain unchanged.

changes in demand An increase in demand takes place when customers wish to buy a greater quantity than previously of a particular good or service, at whatever price it is obtainable. Supply may be slow to adjust itself to such a change. The immediate effect, therefore, is for the market equilibrium price of the commodity to rise. A decrease in demand causes the reverse.

cheap money Descriptive of a period or a government monetary policy in which the interest rates charged on loans are well below average.

choice A necessity arising because all resources are insufficient to produce the quantities of goods and services required to satisfy all needs. The consumer must choose because his income and the prevailing prices limit the amount of goods and services he can buy. The manufacturer must decide what, how, when and where to produce. The state must decide on the best deployment of the limited resources of the nation in the light of national priorities.

circular flow of income A highly simplified model of the working of an economy. Spending by individuals on goods and services gives firms their income. This in turn is paid out to individuals as their incomes in the form of wages, interest, dividends, fees and profit. This is then respent on goods, and so on. There are withdrawals (or leakages) from, and injections into, this circular flow.

circular flow of income—injections into New money being pumped into the circular flow. This comes from capital investment by firms including increases in stocks and the amount of work in progress, government spending on goods, subsidies, transfer payments and interest, and income from abroad in payment for exports.

circular flow of income—withdrawals from Parts of income which are not passed on as spending on goods and services. These include savings made by individuals or by firms in the form of undistributed profits, taxes paid by individuals and firms and money spent abroad on imports.

closed economy A simplified model of an economy which is assumed to be self-sufficient so that it has no exports or imports. It gives a starting point for examining the factors determining the level of an economy's national income free from the complications of international trade.

collective goods Public goods.

collusion An explicit or implicit agreement among firms in an industry to co-operate in order to avoid mutually damaging competition.

command economy A centrally controlled economy.

commerce That sector of the productive process that is concerned with the distribution of raw materials to manufacturers, and with the distribution of finished goods to the consumer via the wholesale and retail trades. It thus embraces all forms of trade, and the supporting services of transport, insurance and banking.

comparative advantage The advantage that one country has over another country if, by reallocating resources from another line of production, it is able to produce a given quantity of a particular good with less sacrifice of the alternative output than would be the case in the other country.

comparative costs Comparative advantage.

compensating income change The sum of money by which a person's income would have to be be increased to offset a price rise so as to enable him to continue to buy the combination of goods and services that he bought prior to the price rise.

compensation principle A criterion by which to decide whether the implementation of a proposed economic change would increase or decrease total social welfare. Virtually all economic policy measures involve making some people better off and others worse off. If it would be possible for the beneficiaries to fully compensate the losers, and still be better off than they were before the change, then the change should be implemented.

competition The action when a firm attempts to win over customers from its rival firms, while retaining its existing customers. It does this through price competition and/or non-price competition. The former involves offering its product at a price lower than those of its rivals. The latter involves trying to increase its share of the market while leaving the price of its product unchanged, by persuading customers of the superiority or advantages associated with its product. It employs techniques such as advertising, the introduction of new brands, self-identifying labelling, attractive packaging, gift schemes and competitions, establishing a reputation for quality or for efficient after-sales services, etc.

competitive demand The nature of the demand for two goods that are fairly good substitutes for one another (butter and margarine). A rise in the price of one causes some degree of switch to the substitute. A rise in the quantity demanded of one will reduce the quantity demanded of the substitute. To some extent all goods are in competitive demand with one another because the purchase of more of one necessitates the purchase of less of the others.

competitive goods Substitutes.

competitive market One in which any individual buyer or seller is handling quantities of the goods that form only a very small proportion of the total being traded in a given period. Consequently he is aware that, as one small trader among many, he can have no influence on the price of the goods which he accepts as the ruling market price.

complementary demand When the amount bought of one good affects the amount bought of another because they are used in association with each other. A rise in the price of one will reduce the amount consumed, and will also reduce the amount consumed of its complement. A change in the popularity and hence the quantity demanded of one generally causes a prportionate change in the quantity demanded of the other.

complementary goods Goods which, as a result of consumer taste or technical relationship are used in conjunction with each other.

composite demand The total demand for a raw material that is used as a component in the manufacture of several different final products. An increase in the demand for one purpose reduces the amount of the raw material available for the others.

composite supply The total supply of a number of competitive products which satisfy a particular demand. An example is tea, coffee and cocoa which supply the demand for hot beverages.

concentration (1) The degree to which a relatively small number of firms account for a significant proportion of the output of an industry or of the demand for an industry's products. (2) The degree to which an industry has become localised within a particular area.

concentration ratio A measure of the extent of the dominating market influence of a few major firms in an industry. It is expressed as the percentage of the total industry sales or employment attributable to the largest three, four, five or more firms.

conglomerate A business organisation consisting of a holding company and a group of subsidiary companies each of which may produce a separate and dissimilar range of products.

constant returns to scale The situation experienced by a firm, undertaking an expansion of productive capacity and output, when it finds that its long-run average cost of production are the same at all levels of output. This happens when the increase in its manpower, plant and machinery, raw materials, etc. causes total production costs to increase by x per cent, and this is matched by an increase of exactly x per cent in the total output of the factory.

consumer The individual, household, group or organisation that buys and uses a final good or service.

consumer durable A relatively expensive household good, such as a refrigerator or a piece of furniture, which is not immediately used up but gives service for several years.

consumer equilibrium The theoretical situation in which the consumer allocates the spending of his disposable income to obtain that combination of goods and services where the marginal utility (satisfaction) per pound spent on each is equal.

consumer goods Goods which have passed through all stages of manufacture and are in the final form in which they will be bought by the private individuals who wish to make use of them.

consumer sovereignty The extent to which consumers, collectively exercising freedom of choice in a free market, are the dominant influence on the pattern of supply and, in the long run, the allocation of productive resources. By buying in varying amounts their freely chosen items from a competing range of goods, they indicate to the manufacturers their preferences as to the type, quality and quantity of goods that they wish to be made available. Manufacturers have no choice but to respond to the consumers' wishes as expressed through the markets.

consumer surplus The difference between the price actually paid by a consumer for a commodity and the higher price that he would be willing to pay rather than do without that purchase. It is a measure of the benefit received from a commodity in excess of the amount paid for it.

consumption The act of using goods and services for the meeting of needs.

consumption expenditure (1) That part of the national expenditure spent on consumer goods and services. It includes the personal expenditure of individuals and the expenditure of central and local public authorities on these items. (2) That part of a person's disposable income spent on goods and services.

consumption function A schedule which lists for each of a series of income levels the amount of that income that would be spent on consumption goods. It may show the relationship between disposable personal income and personal consumption spending, or for a country, the relationship between national income and aggregate consumption expenditure.

controlled market One over which public authorities exercise substantial direct control by licensing buyers and sellers or by setting legal minimum or maximum prices or quotas at which trading can take place.

cost benefit analysis A method of deciding whether to proceed with a proposed investment project by comparing its projected total financial and social gains and losses to the community It attempts to evaluate all the financial and non-monetary benefits and costs of all people and firms who would be affected directly or indirectly if the project were carried out. It takes into account the possible detrimental or beneficial effects on people's environment, lifestyle, travel facilities, etc. and on the activities of firms within the area affected.

cost curve A curve joining points plotted on a graph which indicate the costs which a firm would incur in achieving different levels of output. Separate cost curves are often constructed on the same graph to show the relationship of specific types of cost such as total costs, fixed costs and variable costs.

cost minimisation The employment of the most efficient way to produce a given output by selecting that combination of capital equipment, manpower and other productive resources that could produce the output at the least cost.

cost of living index A retail price index.

cost-push inflation Inflation which is initiated and sustained by firms' rising costs of production, particularly payments for higher wages and salaries, increased power or raw material costs, or a rise in the prices of essential imports.

cost schedule A table relating total, fixed and variable costs of production to given levels of output. From this information, scedules of marginal costs and average costs can be developed.

costs of production The expenses a firm has to incur in order to obtain the resources required for the manufacture of a product or the provision of a service. These include payments for rent, mortgages, interest on loans, dividends, salaries and wages, maintenance and replacement of plant and machinery, raw materials, power, fuel, etc.

costs of production—effect on price Costs of production have no immediate influence on the price of a commodity since people will only pay for it a price which coincides with their estimate of its worth. Costs do, however, have a long-term influence since they curtail or expand long-term supply. If the price people are willing to pay is well above the cost of production, the resulting high profits will attract new producers into the industry. The addition to the supply will reduce the price until it is equal to the cost of production. Conversely, if the price people are prepared to pay is below the cost of production, this will drive firms out of the market and reduce supply until a rising price once again equals cost.

credit (1) In the strict economic sense, types of lending that cause an increase in the money supply because they are not effected by lending the deposits of one person or firm to another and hence are not matched by a counterbalancing reduction in deposits. (2) In the commercial sense, the facility to acquire goods 'on credit', that is, without immediate payment.

credit creation   The process whereby a bank can increase its lending providing it limits the total value of its lending to a particular multiple of the value of its cash reserves. The bank simply credits the borrower's account with the amount of the loan. Thus the money supply in the form of bank deposits on current account is increased.

credit multiplier   The percentage change in the total amount of money lent by a bank once it has had time to fully respond to a one per cent change in the value of its cash reserves.

credit restriction   A government-imposed monetary policy to reduce the amount of credit extended to customers by banks, higher purchase companies and other financial organisations.

credit squeeze   Credit restriction.

creditor nation   A country with a balance of payments surplus.

creeping inflation   A gradual but nevertheless persistent rise in the general price level.

cross elasticity of demand   A measure of the relationship between two goods when the quantity demanded of one good responds to a change in the price of the other. It is measured by dividing the percentage change in the quantity demanded of the first good by the percentage change in price of the second good. The result is positive for substitute goods, negative for complementary goods and zero for unrelated goods.

currency   (1) The notes and coins of a country's money supply. (2) The unit of account of a country. (3) Foreign money held in bank balances for use in financing international transactions.

currency appreciation An increase in the value or exchange rate of one currency in terms of other currencies. Each unit of currency exchanges for more dollars, francs, etc.

currency depreciation A fall in the value or exchange rate of one currency in terms of other currencies. Each unit of currency exchanges for fewer dollars, francs, etc.

currency revaluation The deliberate raising by the government of the value of its country's currency in terms of foreign currencies. Each unit of its currency exchanges for more dollars, francs, etc.

current account A bank account on which a customer may issue cheques up to the amount of the balance on the account, or beyond it to an agreed overdraft limit.

current assets A firm's assets in the form of either cash or items which will soon become cash. These include the firm's stock of raw materials, semi-finished and finished goods, the total of debts owing to it, and its cash in hand and at the bank.

current expenditure Expenditure on regularly recurring items such as wages, rates, interest, electricity, raw materials, etc.

customs union A group of countries between whom there is an agreement to allow each other free trade but to place a common external tariff on goods imported from countries outside the group.

cyclical unemployment Unemployment resulting from the decline of economic activity in the downswing of a trade cycle. It is characterised by a general deficiency of demand, so that nearly all industries are affected at the same time.

Dd

data Statistical information on population, employment, market and financial matters that has been collected, analysed and published by government departments, commercial and industrial associations, trade unions and other research agencies. Examples are: the age distribution of the population, the distribution of income, the per capita gross national product of different countries, the shares of the five largest firms in the markets of specified commodities, the combined accounts of the UK public enterprises, the balance of payments accounts, the retail price index.

dear money Descriptive of a period or a government monetary policy in which the interest rates charged on loans are well above average.

debtor nation One with a balance of payments deficit.

decentralised economy One in which production and consumption decisions are not made by central planners but are taken by individual firms and households through the operation of the free market price mechanism.

decision lag The delay in time between the recognition of the need for action in response to an economic situation, and the taking of the policy decision.

decreasing cost industry One that is in that phase of an expansion programme where it experiences a continuous reduction in average total cost per unit of output.

decreasing returns to scale Diseconomies of scale.

deficit An excess of expenditure flow over income flow for a given period, or where liabilities exceed assets at a given point of time.

deficit financing A deliberately budgeted excess of government expenditure over income with the object of stimulating economic activity and employment by injecting more purchasing power into the economy. The excess spending is financed by borrowing.

deflation A curtailment of the money supply which results in a reduction of the level of economic activity in an economy. It is accompanied by lower levels of national income, employment, imports, lower rates of increases of wages and prices, and an increase in the purchasing power of money.

deflationary gap The amount by which a country's present level of total spending on goods and services would have to rise in order to generate an upsurge in the level of economic activity and national income of sufficient size to absorb the existing pool of unemployed workers and give full employment.

deindustrialisation A tendency over time for an increasing proportion of a country's productive resources to be found in businesses and local and central government organisations concerned with the provision of services, and for the proportion in the extractive and manufacturing industries to fall.

demand The quantity of a good or service that customers are willing and able to buy per unit of time at a particular price. It is usually true that the quantity demanded of a good falls if its price increases, and vice versa.

demand curve A curve joining points plotted on a graph from the information contained in a demand schedule. It indicates the quantity of a product that will be bought per unit of time at each of a range of prices per unit of the product.

demand curve—shift of If the state of demand changes, that is if more or fewer goods are demanded at any given price than formerly, a new demand curve will need to be drawn either to the left or to the right of the existing curve. This is described as a shift of the existing curve to the left or the right. A shift to the right indicates an increase in demand, that is a change in the quantity demanded at each and every price, and a shift to the left indicates a decrease.

demand-deficient unemployment That which occurs because of a simultaneous reduction in the demand for many goods. Total demand is insufficient to purchase all the output that could be produced by a fully employed labour force. There is an excess of workers looking for jobs over the number of jobs available.

demand for labour The factors affecting a firm's recruitment of workers. It will wish to increase its workforce to such a size that the contribution to revenue made by the last worker taken on just equals the cost of his wages. This marginal revenue depends upon the increase in physical output and the extra revenue from the sale of the increase. The former depends upon the marginal productivity of the manpower and the latter on the elasticity of the demand for the product.

demand for money The extent to which people and firms prefer to hold higher proportions of their assets in the form of cash, notes and non-interest earning bank deposits instead of as investments in securities earning interest or dividends. To hold assets as money involves the loss of the return they would otherwise have earned.

demand function The extent and way in which the quantity of a good that a consumer wants to buy is a function of, or varies according to, any one of a number of factors. These include the price of the good, the prices of complementary goods and substitutes, the size of the consumer's income, and his tastes and habits. By holding all these factors constant except one, we can study the relationship between quantity demanded and this one factor by observing how the former varies with changes in the latter.

demand increase A situation where there is an in increase in the quantity of a good or service that customers are willing to buy at whatever the market price happens to be.

demand price The price at which buyers will be prepared to purchase a given quantity of a good or service per day, week, month, etc.

demand-pull inflation A situation where a country's total demand for goods and services is constantly running ahead of the national output. This results in rising prices and scarcities of manpower and materials.

demand schedule A table stating, for a given state of demand, the quantity of a commodity per day, week, month, etc, that buyers would be prepared to purchase at each of a range of prices.

demand theory The branch of economics that analyses the determinants of a consumer's choice of a particular set of purchases from all those that are open to him. They include the consumer's tastes and habits, his income and the prices of the goods. There is an underlying assumption that the consumer, within the limitations imposed by his income, seeks that combination of goods and services that gives him the greatest satisfaction.

demographic unemployment Unemployment caused by an increase in the supply of workers due to more of them entering the labour market than retire from it. The cause may be a change in the age structure of the population, later retirement or the result of changes in social conditions such as more married women seeking employment.

denationalisation Privatisation.

deposit money The largest part of the money supply. It consists of deposits in bank current accounts. Since cheques drawn against such deposits are a generally accepted means of exchange, the deposits are regarded as money.

depreciation—accounting That part of the original cost of an item of plant or machinery that is charged, when calculating profit, as the loss in its value resulting from its use during a year. Since such capital items will last for several years, a firm will not include their full cost in the year of purchase, but will spread such cost over several successive years.

depreciation—economic Wastages arising from worn-out or obsolescent plant and equipment and from depleted stock levels of raw materials and unfinished and finished goods. These must be made good in order to avoid a reduction in capital stock.

depression A prolonged trough of the trade cycle typified by widespread unemployment, a low demand for consumer and producer goods and services, the stagnation of much of the potential productive capacity of industry, low profits, closures of firms, absence of confidence in the future, firms unwilling to risk new investments, and a low level of borrowing.

derived demand A demand that exists only as a result of another demand. The need of a firm for each of the various types of productive inputs that it requires, such as employees, land, buildings, machinery, equipment and raw materials, arises solely out of the demand for the goods or services which the firm produces with their help.

deterioration in the terms of trade This happens if the average price of a country's imports increases relative to the average price of its exports. This implies that the country can buy a smaller quantity of imports with the money obtained by selling a given quantity of exports.

devaluation Cheapening the value internationally of a country's money. A deliberate reduction of the official exchange rate at which one country's currency is exchanged for others. One unit of the devalued currency now exchanges for fewer units than before of all other currencies. As a result imports into the devaluing country are dearer and so tend to be reduced, and exports out of the devaluing country are cheaper to other countries and so tend to increase.

developing nations Countries with a very low gross national product per head of the population due to the presence of one or more barriers to economic development which they are attempting to overcome. Such barriers could be a shortage of natural resources, population expansion outstripping national output expansion, technical inefficiency in the use of resources, poor health and education, lack of managerial skills, lack of access to or the ability to generate financial investment, insufficient industrial capacity, an adverse climate.

diminishing marginal returns, law of This states that while increasing one input in a productive process by small constant amounts (all other inputs being held constant) may at first cause output per unit of time to increase, after some point the increases in output will become smaller. Ultimately successive inputs of the variable factor will result in a less than proportionate increase in output. In the extreme, further additions will become counter-productive and total output will fall.

diminishing marginal utility Beyond a certain point, the larger a person's consumption or supply of a commodity within a given period, the less utility or satisfaction he derives from an extra unit of it. While each extra unit increases his supply and adds to total utility, it nevertheless adds less utility than the previous one. Although each extra unit is identical, its marginal utility depends on the size of the consumer's existing supply or the amount he has already consumed.

direct costs Variable costs.

direct tax A tax which is assessed on the income or wealth of an individual or a firm.

discriminating monopoly One that can sell the same product at different prices to different customers. It is able to separate its customers into sub-groups (or sub-markets) who each have a different elasticity of demand for the product. It can then charge a profit-maximising price within each sub-group, charging a higher price to those customers who

distribution of income

are prepared to pay such a price. This is possible only when the sub-groups obtaining the product at a lower price are prevented by space or time restrictions from re-selling it to the higher price sub-groups.

diseconomies of scale When higher output causes even higher costs. The rise in the average total cost of a unit of its product encountered by a firm beyond some stage of a long-run period of expansion. Expansion of output of x per cent causes total production costs to increase by more than x per cent.

disinflation A deliberate policy of reducing inflationary pressure on the economy in order to maintain the purchasing power of money. It is achieved by direct restriction of consumer spending by hire purchase controls, the creation of a budget surplus, the raising of interest rates and credit squeezes.

disinvestment This occurs when capital assets such as plant and equipment are not replaced as they wear out, or when firms run down their stocks of raw materials or semi-finished and finished goods.

disposable personal income A person's gross income less any compulsory deductions. The income actually available for spending or saving. It is calculated by deducting from total income from all sources, including transfer payments, all direct taxes and national insurance contributions.

dissaving Spending past savings. To finance an excess of spending over disposable income, assets accumulated by past saving are drawn upon and hence diminished.

distribution of income The shareout of the national income. The proportion of the national income received by different groups of the population. The groups may be selected on the basis of the source of the income from rent, interest, profits, etc. or to show allocation between various social or economic groupings.

distribution of income theory Economic theory concerned with the factors affecting payments of rent, wages, interest and profit to the owners of productive resources for their share in the work of production, and with the factors determining the share of the national income received by each person. It seeks to explain the way in which the total flow of goods and services available for consumption is distributed among people in the economy.

disutility The opposite of utility, or negative utility. It arises when, within a given period, consumption of additional units of a good does not add to the total satisfaction but, on the contrary, begins to detract from it. The extra units cause loss of benefit in the form of inconvenience or over-satiation.

diversification of industry A planned increase in the variety of industries operating within a particular area in order to reduce reliance upon one or two dominant industries which may be in decline. Its objective is to create more stable and expanding employment opportunities.

diversification of products This occurs when a firm undertakes production of a new product without ceasing production of its present products. It may take place by acquisition of a firm which manufactures the product into which diversification is sought. There are usually close technological or marketing links between the existing and the new products.

division of labour Specialisation of the manpower input to a production process of a particular commodity. The entire process is broken down into separate operations and each worker does one operation which may be a small fraction of the total necessary to produce the commodity.

domestic product at factor cost The value of the domestic product at market prices adjusted to eliminate the effects of taxes and subsidies. The market price of a good or service includes any tax levied on it by the government. If any of these taxes are increased, there is an increase in market prices and hence the value of the domestic product as measured by expenditure, even if the quantities of goods and services bought are unchanged. Subsidies have the reverse effect. To compensate for this, taxes are excluded from the total expenditure and subsidies are added back.

domestic product at market prices The total value of all goods and services produced in a country in a given year, the goods and services being valued at the price the customer pays for them.

double counting An error that would arise if the domestic product were calculated by adding up the sales of all firms at all levels of production. This would produce a total greatly in excess of the value of the finished goods sold to the final customers. This is because at each inter-firm sale down the chain of production, the price includes the cost to the seller of raw materials and intermediate goods required for their manufacture. These costs would be included repeatedly in the prices charged at subsequent sales as the goods move closer to the retail level.

dumping The sale of a commodity on a foreign market at a price below the cost of producing it. An exporting firm, with or without government subsidy, may pursue this policy in order to eliminate competition, to break into a new market or to dispose of temporary surpluses without causing a reduction in home prices.

duopoly A market situation in which the good or service involved can be obtained from one or the other of only two sellers.

duopsony A market situation in which the good or service involved can be sold to one or the other of only two buyers.

durable good One such as a building or a piece of machinery that is not used up within a short time of being purchased but yields its services over an extended period of time.

Ee

easy money policy A monetary policy, designed to stimulate economic activity, which creates conditions where money can be easily and cheaply borrowed. It is implemented by lowering interest rates, increasing the quantity of money in circulation, relaxing restrictions on lending, and making less stringent the controlled conditions on hire purchase.

econometrics A specialised branch of mathematical and statistical techniques used to develop and to test economic theories.

economic growth The long-run increase in a country's output of goods and services. The rate of economic growth is obtained by comparing the actual output of goods and services from one year to another, adjustments having been made for changes in prices.

economic indicators Statistics which give guidance on the nature and extent of changes in the state of industry, trade and commerce. Examples are statistics of unemployment, bank advances, gold reserve, basic materials and fuel prices, retail prices, wage rates, retail sales, imports and exports.

economic life The period from the installation of a building, plant or piece of equipment up to the point when its obsolescence renders it an uneconomic asset to retain, although it has not reached the end of its physical life.

economic model A theory which attempts to explain what and how factors determine economic phenomena such as price, income, output levels, choice, etc. It proceeds by selecting from real-life experience only those factors considered essential to the argument. This is because in the complex reality of economic life many associated factors are continually changing, and in order to understand any one aspect, it is necessary to isolate it and presume other factors to remain constant.

economic rent That part of the payment to a factor of production which is in excess of the minimum amount required to retain it in its present employment or use.

economic sanction A measure taken in respect of some economic activity, which has the effect of damaging another country's economy. Examples are a partial or complete embargo on trade between countries or refusing to permit the government and residents of the target country to draw on bank deposits held in the sanction-imposing country.

economic system The way in which a country's economic activities are organised, and in particular to what extent it is a free-market economy or a centrally-controlled economy.

economic welfare Those aspects of social welfare that are concerned with people's material standard of living as measured by their consumption of goods and services, as distinct from their bodily, moral and spiritual well-being.

economics The study of (1) the methods by which the scarce productive resources of a society are allocated among the industries competing for their use, (2) the factors affecting firms in their use of resources in producing goods and services, (3) the forces influencing the distribution of the output of these productive resources among individuals or groups, (4) the ways in which production and distribution change over time, and (5) the efficiencies and inefficiencies of economic systems.

economies of scale These occur in a firm undertaking a long-run expansion of its productive capacity, when each increase in output is produced with a less than proportionate increase in total costs. Long-run average total costs per unit of output are thus decreasing.

economy An alternative name for a country when one wishes to consider it collectively as an economic organisation.

effective demand A term used only when it is necessary to distinguish 'demand' from 'need'. Demand for things is restricted because people have only a limited amount of money to spend. The mere need for a good or service does not become a purchase unless there is the ability and willingness to pay a sum of money for some amount of it.

elastic demand The state of demand for a good or service when a slight rise or fall in its price produces a more than proportionate change in the amount of it people are able and willing to buy.

elastic supply The state of demand for a good or service when a slight rise or fall in its price produces a more than proportionate change in the amount of it firms are able and willing to supply.

elasticity A measure of the degree of responsiveness of one variable to a change in another. The elasticity of y with respect to x is the percentage positive or negative change in the size of y caused by a 1 per cent change in the size of x.

elasticity of demand The degree of responsiveness of the quantity demanded of a good to a change in its price. It is measured by dividing the percentage change in the quantity demanded by the percentage price change. If this gives a result larger than 1, demand is elastic. If it is less than 1, demand is inelastic. If it is exactly 1, demand is unitary.

elasticity of demand—substitutes The most important influence on elasticity of demand is whether there are close substitutes for the good or service within the same price range. A price rise encourages the purchaser to turn to a substitute. The closer the substitutes, the more elastic is likely to be the demand. If there are no close substitutes, demand is likely to be inelastic.

elasticity of demand—luxuries and necessities Whether goods are luxuries or necessities is not the chief determinant of elasticity of demand if they have close substitutes. If there are no close substitutes, the extent to which the commodity is a necessity will increase the inelasticity of the demand for it.

elasticity of demand for productive resources The extent to which a firm's demand for productive resources such as buildings, new machinery, raw materials or manpower is influenced by their price. This will depend upon the elasticity of demand for the final product they help to make, the amount of the resource required and the ease with which one resource can be substituted for another.

elasticity of substitution of commodities A measure of the ease or difficulty with which consumers can substitute between commodities. It is calculated by dividing the percentage change in the ratio in which two commodities are combined by the percentage change in the ratio of their marginal utilities. A high value indicates a high degree of substitutability, and vice versa.

elasticity of substitution of productive resources A measure of the ease or difficulty with which firms can substitute between productive resources. It is measured by dividing the percentage change in the ratio in which two resources are combined by the percentage change in the ratio of their marginal physical productivities. A high value indicates a high degree of technical substitutability between resources, and vice versa.

elasticity of supply A measure of the responsiveness of the quantity supplied of a commodity to a change in the price of the commodity. It is measured by dividing the percentage change in quantity supplied by the percentage change in price that brought it about. Supply is elastic if this value is greater than 1, inelastic if it is less than 1, and unitary if it is exactly 1.

entrepreneur The managing proprietor of a firm who supplies the capital, bears the risks of production and controls a firm. He decides what goods to produce, what scale of production to adopt, is responsible for the setting up of the firm and for the combination and co-ordination of the productive resources in optimum proportion. He undertakes the day-to-day management and the marketing of the goods, and decides the development policy. Other than in the smallest companies, there is no single entrepreneur, the above functions being divided between shareholders, boards of directors and salaried executives.

equilibrium concept A theoretical situation in which forces making for change in opposing directions are perfectly balanced so that there is no incentive for anyone to alter the way in which he behaves in order to benefit from a feasible change in the situation.

equilibrium distribution of spending Purchasing just so much of each of a number of goods and services that the marginal utility per pound spent on each is equal.

equilibrium firm A firm in the situation when the maximum profit is being earned and there is no incentive to increase or decrease output.

equilibrium industry An industry in the situation when the margin of profit is such that there is no tendency for firms to enter or leave the industry.

equilibrium level of national income That level at which the national income exhibits no tendencies to either increase or decrease. This is when the contractionary force exerted by saving is just equal to the expansionary force exerted by investment.

equilibrium market A market is in equilibrium when at the ruling price the amount of goods or services being offered for sale is just matched by the amount consumers wish to buy.

equilibrium price The price of a good or service when market conditions of supply and demand have had time to settle down so that the rate at which it is offered for sale is just matched by the rate at which it is purchased.

equilibrium quantity The quantity of a good or service which is bought and sold at the equilibrium price.

excess capacity The operating situation of a firm or industry when actual output is below the level at which all its productive resources are fully employed. Production is at too low a rate to exploit economies of scale to the full.

excess demand A situation in which the quantity of a good or service which buyers wish to buy at the prevailing price exceeds that which sellers are prepared to sell. It occurs when the market price is below the equilibrium price. This causes buyers to bid up the price, so inducing an increase in the quantity offered for sale and a decrease in the quantity demanded. Price will continue to rise until excess demand is eliminated.

excess supply A situation in which the quantity of a good or service which sellers wish to sell at the prevailing price exceeds the quantity which buyers wish to buy. This occurs when the market price is above the equilibrium price. This causes sellers to bid down the price, thus causing an increase in the quantity demanded and a decrease in the quantity offered for sale. Price will continue to fall until excess supply is eliminated.

exchange Trade.

exchange control Government intervention on the foreign exchange market to control balance of payments situations. It is carried out by buying or selling its own currency, or by imposing restrictions on the overseas movement of funds and on dealings in gold and foreign currency by its own people.

exchange equalisation account An account controlled by the Treasury and managed by the Bank of England which buys and sells sterling for gold and foreign currencies with the object of offsetting major fluctuations in the exchange value of the pound.

exchange rate The number of units of one currency that can be exchanged for one unit of another currency.

expansion of trade Trade recovery.

expectations Attitudes, beliefs or states of mind about the possible trend of future events that affect current economic decisions.

expected future capital yield A factor which influences the level of investment. For investment to take place, this yield must be greater than the rate of interest that would have to be paid on money borrowed for investment.

expenditure share The fraction of total consumption expenditure spent on a particular good or service in a given period. It is calculated by multiplying the unit price of the good by the quantity of units purchased and then expressing this as a percentage of total consumption expenditure.

export multiplier The effect on a country's national income of a rise or fall in its exports. A rise in exports is an increase in demand for home-produced goods which gives extra income in the form of wages, rent, profit, etc. to those associated with the exporting firms. They will save some of this extra income and spend the rest. This spending will in its turn generate extra incomes. Again the recipients will save some and spend the rest. This process will repeat itself, its effect diminishing with each round because part of the income is saved instead of being passed on in spending. When it has worked itself through, it will have caused an expansion in incomes which is several times greater than the originating export rise. A fall in exports will produce the reverse effect.

export price index Price index of exports.

exports The goods or services sold by one country to the resident individuals, firms or public authorities of another country, the transactions involving international payments.

external economies and diseconomies External effects.

external effects The uninvited effects, beneficial or otherwise, on the welfare of individuals or the production activities of firms, caused by the consumption activities of another individual or the production activities of another firm. They are the social implications which are not taken into account in the financial cost calculations of the consumption or production activity.

externalities External effects.

extractive industries Those such as mining, quarrying, forestry, agriculture and fishing which draw out from land and water the raw materials provided by the forces of nature, and process them to a state in which they can be sold to the manufacturing sector of industry.

Ff

factor cost The selling price of a good or service adjusted by deducting any tax that has inflated it and by adding back any subsidy that has reduced it. This is the amount actually received by the firm for payment to the factors that have contributed to the production of the good or service.

factor demand curve A curve joining the points on a graph which plot the quantity of a factor of production that a firm or an industry will be willing to buy or hire at each of a range of prices per unit of the factor.

factor endowment The quantity and quality available in a country of each of the four factors of production, land, labour, capital and entrepreneurship.

factor incomes Payments of wages, salaries, rent, interest and profits made to factors of production for the services that they render to the productive process.

factor markets Markets through which the services of factors of production are bought and sold. The factor may be defined in general terms (the labour market or the property market) or in more specific terms (the market for building trade workers or the commercial property market).

factor mobility The ease or difficulty with which factors of production can be transferred from one use to another in response to factor price changes.

factor payments Factor incomes.

factor proportions The ratio in which factors of production are combined in a particular production process.

fiscal policy

factor supply curve A curve joining the points on a graph which plot the quantity of a factor of production that the factor owners will be willing to sell or lease to firms in response to each of a range of prices per unit of the factor.

factors of production The resources or inputs which combine in a productive process to give an output of goods and services. Their traditional classification has been into the broad groups of land, labour, capital and entrepreneurship.

favourable balance of trade The situation when the value of a country's exports is greater than that of its imports, that is, when there is a balance of trade surplus.

final goods Goods which have passed through all stages of production and are in the final form in which they are purchased by the consumer for direct use. They are to be distingished from producer or intermediate goods which are bought by firms to feed into a process which will change their form to enable them to contribute to the production of some other good.

financial intermediary An organisation such as a bank, building society or insurance company which acts as a link between those who save money and those who wish to borrow it.

firm The unit that employs the services of factors of production to produce goods or services that it sells to other firms, to individuals or to public authorities.

firm's short-run supply curve The curve joining the points on a graph which plot the output the firm would be willing to produce with its existing size of plant at each of a range of prices.

fiscal policy The use by the government of the amount and nature of its taxation and its expenditure to help diminish fluctuations in the level of the country's economic activity. This involves either budget deficits or budget surpluses, which raise or lower the level of the country's spending on goods and services.

fixed assets A firm's non-financial assets such as buildings and machinery which are relatively long-lived and specific to a particular productive process. Their cost is recoverable only over an operating period of several years' duration.

fixed costs Costs which in the short run do not vary with the level of output. They include such costs as the rent of the premises or interest payments on loans. These would still have to be paid even if there were no output.

fixed exchange rate A foreign exchange rate for a country's currency which the government does not allow to vary in response to market forces, other than within certain narrow limits. The country's central bank maintains a buffer stock of gold and foreign currencies which it uses to buy or sell its currency on the foreign exchange market as soon as its price approaches either the lower or upper set limits.

fixed factor of production A factor such as buildings, machinery, land, or a supply of workers with highly specific skills, whose input level cannot be varied in the short run to assist increased production.

fixed supply A short-run situation where the supply of a good or service cannot be altered whatever the price offered by buyers. The prevailing price will accordingly depend on the current intensity of the aggregate demand for the good or service.

flexible exchange rates Exchange rates between national currencies that, free from government intervention, are allowed to fluctuate in response to market forces. These comprise the international demand for and supply of currencies or gold to settle import-export balances.

floating exchange rates Flexible exchange rates.

forced saving Saving achieved through an enforced reduction in the community's consumption of goods and services rather than because consumers wish to save. It may be effected by deliberate government action or by the working of free economic forces. The state may undertake saving on behalf of the community by imposing additional taxation. This curtails consumption and brings in the amount to be saved. In a situation of excess demand, where an increased supply is not possible, prices rise until the excess demand is eliminated by inflation.

foreign currency demand   The need for foreign currencies to pay for imports, the purchase of foreign securities, travel abroad, placing deposits in foreign bank accounts, incomes to residents in other countries, interest to foreign lenders, dividends to foreign shareholders, financing investment projects overseas and making gifts abroad.

foreign exchange market   The market in which transactions are conducted to effect the transfer of currency of one country into that of another. The market is not located in a single country but is international, its transactions being conducted through world communication links.

foreign investment   Any expenditure by individuals or firms on the acquisition or creation of buildings, plant or any other installation in another country, or on purchasing foreign securities.

forward integration   The action of a firm in extending the range of its activities into lower stages of the production process. A manufacturing concern may decide to establish or acquire a retail organisation in order to ensure secure outlets for its products.

free exchange rates   Flexible exchange rates.

free market   One in which the forces of supply and demand are allowed to operate unhampered by government intervention.

free market economy   The theoretical concept of an economy in which all production is free from government control. The allocation of resources is determined by sales and purchase decisions taken by firms and consumers in response to the interaction of supply and demand conditions prevailing in individual markets. Consumers have a free choice as to what they buy, limited only by the amount of money they have to spend. The relative strength of the consumers' demands for various goods or services ultimately determines the amount of each that entrepreneurs will try to produce. In practice, no economies are entirely free. It is a question of degree. In some economies the influence of the government is substantially less than in others.

free trade The condition in which the free flow of goods and services is neither restricted nor encouraged by direct government intervention through artificial barriers such as tariffs, quotas on imports or subsidies on exports.

free trade area An association of countries between whom there has been a removal of all import tariffs and quotas and export subsidies and other measures to influence trade. Each country however continues to retain its own international trade controls when dealing with countries outside the association.

freedom of entry The absence of any restriction to prevent any individual or group from setting up a firm to trade in a particular good or service in an existing market.

freely floating exchange rates Flexible exchange rates.

frictional unemployment Interim short-term unemployment resulting from the time lag involved in the redeployment of labour. Even if there is a job available for everyone who wants one, it takes time for a person moving from one job to another to find a vacancy, be interviewed and be taken on. At any one time there will always be a small pool of unemployment owing to these frictions in the working of the labour market.

full cost pricing A method of fixing the price of a good by adding a profit margin (or markup) onto its average total cost per unit of production. The average total cost per unit is calculated on the basis of what the firm regards as the normal capacity output of the plant.

functional distribution of income

full employment A situation in which all those seeking work in a community are able to find suitable work fairly readily. To achieve this, the number of unfilled vacancies must exceed the number of persons seeking work. Full employment does not mean that every person is fully employed all the time, for there will always be at any one moment some frictional unemployment because of the time it takes to change from one job to another.

full employment budget An estimate of the surplus or deficit which would have to be achieved in a government's budget in order to enable the economy to function with full employment at full potential output.

full employment national income An estimate of the potential total value of the output of goods and services that a country would be capable of producing if all its productive resources were fully utilised.

functional distribution of income The national income analysed according to its source as wages and salaries, rent, interest, dividends and profit. It indicates the share earned through personal services (earned income) and that through the ownership of resources (unearned income).

Gg

galloping inflation Hyperinflation.

GDP Gross domestic product

Giffen good A foodstuff of relatively low quality which forms an important part of the diet of low-income households. Contrary to the normal rule, the demand for such a good increases when its price rises and decreases when it falls. A price rise forces households to reduce their consumption of other foods and buy more of the Giffen good to maintain their basic nutritional level. A price reduction causes the opposite effect.

GNP Gross national product.

gold and foreign exchange reserves The stock of gold and foreign currencies held by a country to finance any calls that may be made from its overseas creditors for the settlement of debt.

goods Tangible things that are produced by firms and which individuals want because of the satisfaction they derive from their consumption, or other firms want as an input to their productive processes.

government expenditure That part of public expenditure incurred by the central government as distinct from that incurred by local government authorities and other non-government public agencies.

gross and net output The gross output of a firm is the total selling value of its output within a given period. This includes the value of the necessary materials bought from other firms to produce that output. The net output is found by deducting from the gross output the cost of these incoming supplies. Net

gross national product

output is therefore the value added by the firm's productive process to the cost of the materials used.

gross domestic fixed capital formation The annual increase of a country's stock of industrial, commercial and infrastructure fixed assets situated within the country.

gross domestic product The value of a nation's total output of goods and services produced in one year by factors of production located in the domestic economy, whoever owns them. Also **GDP.**

gross domestic product at constant prices The GDP adjusted to compensate for changes in the value of money when comparing one year with another.

gross domestic product at factor cost Market prices are raised by indirect taxes and and lowered by subsidies. The value of the GDP at market prices will not therefore equal the value of the incomes paid out to the factors of production contributing to the output, namely the GDP at factor cost. This is found by subtracting from the GDP at market prices the total of indirect taxes and then adding the total of subsidies.

gross domestic product at market prices The GDP valued at prices in which no adjustment is made for the fact that they have been raised by indirect taxes and lowered by subsidies.

gross investment Spending on the replacement of worn-out and obsolescent buildings, machinery and equipment and on increasing the stock of such capital assets. It is thus equal to the sum of replacement investment and net investment.

gross national product The GDP plus incomes of domestic residents received from abroad as salaries, dividends or interest minus similar payments made to residents of other countries. Also **GNP.**

gross national product at factor cost Market prices are raised by indirect taxes and and lowered by subsidies. The value of the GNP at market prices will not therefore equal the value of the incomes paid out to the factors of production contributing to the output, namely the GNP at factor cost. This is found by subtracting from the GNP at market prices the total of indirect taxes and then adding the total of subsidies.

gross national product at market prices The GNP valued at prices in which no adjustment is made for the fact that they have been raised by indirect taxes and lowered by subsidies.

Hh

heterogeneous products Goods or services which, although belonging to the same general type, have sufficient individual characteristics to make them non-identical in the eyes of the buyers.

high-powered money The monetary base.

historical cost The cost incurred at the time of the purchase of a productive resource such as a building or a machine. This is is usually less than the current cost of replacing it.

holding money Holding accumulated savings in the form of unappreciating money balances instead of placing them in interest-earning balances or investing them in dividend-paying securities.

homogeneous product One which, although produced by different firms, is undifferentiated and identical in the eyes of the buyer. It is therefore of no consequence from which firm he makes his purchase.

horizontal combination Horizontal integration.

horizontal integration The amalgamation of firms engaged in the same stage of production of the same commodity.

household This consists either of a single person living alone or a group living together. It is an important economic unit when considering the market potential for certain consumer goods, particularly durables, which are sold on the basis of one per household irrespective of the number in the household. It also channels consumer choice for many domestic goods through household as opposed to individual decisions.

human capital Manpower regarded, like physical capital, as a productive resource in which investment can be made. It comprises the skills and knowledge possessed by a worker which enable him to contribute to a firm's output and to earn an income. Training to improve workers' expertise and productivity is an investment in the productive resource of human capital.

hyperinflation Inflation which has got out of control and in which prices rise so rapidly that the economic stability of the country is threatened.

Ii

idle money   That part of the total money supply which has been withdrawn from circulation and is neither being used to finance current transactions nor being lent out on the money market.

IMF   International Monetary Fund.

imperfect competition   A general term for the real-life intermediate market structures which lie between the two theoretical extremes of perfect competition and absolute monopoly. The main types of imperfect competition are monopolistic competition, perfect oligopoly or duopoly, and imperfect oligopoly or duopoly.

imperfect market   The commonly found market structure in which one or more of the theoretical conditions of perfect competition are not fulfilled. There may be few buyers or sellers, a non-homogeneous product, imperfect information on prices, restrictions on entry, buyers or sellers having a significant share of total sales or purchases, or collusion between buyers and between sellers.

implicit costs   The opportunity costs incurred by a producer in placing assets, like a building which he owns, at the disposal of his firm. Such assets, if not used in this way, could have earned him an income in some alternative enterprise. Likewise his own professional skills could have been employed elsewhere for financial gain. The total income foregone by withdrawing these inputs from their most advantageous alternative uses represents the effective cost of using them in the firm.

import duty   An import tariff.

import quota A limit imposed by the government on the quantity of specified goods imported from abroad.

import restrictions Limitations imposed on the quantity or types of goods imported into a country through the use of tariffs or quotas.

import tariff A tax on a good imported into a country. It may be levied on a specific basis as a fixed sum per unit of weight or volume of the imported good, or on an ad valorem basis when it is levied as a percentage of the value of the import.

imported inflation Price rises due to the increased cost of imported raw materials and goods.

imports The goods or services bought by the resident individuals, firms or public authorities of one country from another country, the transactions involving international payments.

improvement in the terms of trade An increase in the average price of a country's exports relative to the average price of its imports. This implies that the country can buy a larger quantity of imports with the money obtained by selling a given quantity of exports.

imputed costs Implicit costs.

imputed rent An estimate of the value of the rent that could otherwise have been obtained for the land or buildings that a firm owns and occupies.

inactive money Idle money.

incidence of indirect taxation How much of the tax on a good or service is paid by the seller and how much by the buyer. This depends on the extent to which the tax can be passed on by the seller to the buyer in the form of a price increase.

income The flow of money accruing to an individual, a firm or other organisation over some period of time. It may originate from the sale of goods or services, from wages, interest, dividends, rent, or from a gift or a transfer payment such as a grant or social security benefit.

income differentials Differences between the average level of incomes in various occupations, industries, social groupings or geographical areas.

income effect of a price change When the price of a good rises, with the consumer's income remaining fixed, the purchasing power of his income is reduced. He will readjust his spending pattern on all goods and services in response to the new relationship between those with unchanged prices and the one with the increased price. This may lead to a rise or fall in the amount bought of the good whose price has changed.

income elastic goods Goods for which a change in the buyer's income causes a more than proportionate change in the amount demanded.

income elasticity of demand The percentage change in the amount demanded of a good at a given price caused by a 1 per cent change in the buyer's income. Goods for which the income elasticity of demand is less than 1 are described as necessities, and those for which it exceeds 1 are described as luxuries.

income inelastic goods Those for which a change in the buyer's income causes a less than proportionate change in the quantity demanded of the good.

income types The classification of income according to whether it is derived from performing personal services or from the ownership of assets. The first type includes wages, salaries, fees, commissions, etc. from personal effort in the form of work. The second type includes rent from leasing land, buildings and equipment, interest from lending money, dividends from shares, or profit from business ownership.

income velocity of circulation The average number of times that the money supply has to circulate round the economy in in order to finance all the transactions that have taken place in one year. It is measured by dividing the value of the national income by the value of the quantity of money in circulation.

incomes policy Government policy aimed at limiting the rate of rise in wages, salaries and other incomes in an attempt to control cost-push inflation.

increase in demand This takes place when there is an increase in the amount of a good or service that buyers are willing and able to buy per day, week, month, etc. at each of a range of prices.

increasing returns to scale Economies of scale.

index number A number which, in varying about a value of 100, enables a straightforward comparison over time in the average value of a set of items. On an agreed base date, the index of the average value of the set of items is set at 100. The average value of the same items at any other time is then expressed as a percentage of their average value at the base date.

index of export prices Price index of exports.

indifference curve The line joining the points on a graph which plot the various combinations by quantity of two goods listed in an indifference schedule. Points on the curve denote combinations that equal each other in the total satisfaction given to the consumer, and accordingly between which he is indifferent.

indifference schedule A theoretical list of different combinations by quantity of two goods, drawn up on the basis that any combination would give the consumer the same satisfaction. He would be indifferent between all these possible combinations, that is, he would feel no better off and no worse off whichever combination he had.

indirect tax A tax levied when a good or service is purchased. It is paid as part of the price. How much indirect tax a person pays depends on the extent to which he uses the good or service. It is possible for him to totally avoid payment by denying himself the use of the good or service.

indivisible factor of production A productive resource such as a large machine which is not divisible into small units and of which the supply cannot therefore be increased gradually. At low output the machine is not fully employed, and if output is increasing there will be economies of scale until the machine is working at full capacity. Any further expansion of output will require the duplication of the machine.

industrial wage differentials Differences in the average level of wages of different groups of workers classified according to the industry in which they are employed.

industrialisation The movement in developing countries to establish industries to home-produce for internal consumption goods that were previously imported, or to produce goods intended for the export market.

industry A group of firms involved directly or indirectly in the production of a given class of goods or services. The range of goods or services to be included is adjustable to the required breadth of classification (e.g. the house-building industry, the building industry, the construction industry).

industry supply schedule A table which lists for each of a range of prices the total quantity of a good that would be supplied at that price by the industry as a whole. It is obtained by adding together the quantities that would be supplied at each price by the individual firms comprising the industry.

ineffective demand A potential demand for goods and services which is currently not backed by the ability of the customers to pay for them, but which would occur if customers' incomes were higher. It cannot therefore express itself to suppliers through the market price mechanism.

inelastic demand The situation when a change in the market price causes a less than proportionate change in the amount demanded.

inelastic supply The situation when a change in the market price causes a less than proportionate change in the amount supplied.

infant industry One that is growing towards its most efficient size and is considered not to be able to withstand foreign competition. It will not operate at an optimum least-cost output until it has reached a sufficient size to obtain significant economies of scale. It will thus be competitively vulnerable in relation to an established industry in a foreign country. Such industries may be afforded the protection of a tariff or granted a subsidy until they are strong enough to stand alone.

inferior good Goods of which less are bought by people in higher income-groups because they can afford to consume superior and hence more expensive substitutes. It is thus a good for which the demand falls when its consumers' incomes rise. It is also one for which demand increases as the prices for both inferior and superior types of the good rise because buyers of limited means are then forced to buy proportionately more of the inferior good.

infinite elasticity Perfect elasticity.

inflation A continuous rise over time in the general price level, which results in the diminishing purchasing power of money.

inflation rate The percentage by which the general level of prices is increasing per year. The prices of different goods and services change at different rates. To enable comparisons to be made between general price levels at different points of time, it is necessary to derive at intervals an average of these many different prices, called the Retail Price Index. The inflation rate is calculated from the annual average of the retail price indices for one year, compared with the annual average for the previous year.

inflationary gap The amount by which total demand for goods and services in the economy exceeds the maximum attainable national output, the total supply of plant, machinery and manpower being fully employed. Firms cannot increase their outputs because they cannot obtain more workers. In competing for the limited supply of workers, they offer higher money wages which in turn further increases demand.

inflationary spiral A situation in which inflation is perpetuated. Firms are able to increase the prices of their goods and services in line with the increases in their costs of production, of which wages and salaries form a large part. Higher prices then lead to demands for cost-of-living rises in wages and salaries. This in turn raises costs of production and so leads to further price increases.

influences on demand The quantity demanded of a good depends on its price, the prices of substitute or complementary goods, the income and wealth of the customers, and current trends or tastes.

infrastructure Services regarded as essential for the development of an economy, such as transportation and communication systems, water supplies, sewage and drainage, electric power, housing, education and health.

input Any good or service such as land, buildings, machinery, materials and manpower that a firm uses in producing an output.

input-output analysis A planning technique of analysing and displaying in tabular form the input requirements of one industry as a share of the output of intermediate goods or raw materials produced by another. From this it is possible to trace the relation between a given set of demands for final goods and services and the implied amounts of inputs that each contributing industry will be required to make to produce these goods and services.

interdependence of demand, supply and price Changes in either supply or demand will affect price. An increase in demand or a decrease in supply will usually raise price. A decrease in demand or an increase in supply will usually lower price. But these are short-term changes which do not allow time for supply to adjust to a new level of demand. In the long run an increase in demand will induce an increase in

interest supply, which may eventually cause a fall in price. Similarly if a decrease in demand induces a contraction in supply, the long-run effect may be a rise in price.

interest The payment made by a borrower to a lender in exchange for the use of an amount of money for an agreed period.

interest-elasticity of the demand for money The percentage reduction in the amount of money demanded for transactionary, precautionary or speculative motives when there is a 1 per cent increase in interest rates.

interest rate Rate of interest.

intermediate demand The demand for a resource or a commodity not for its own sake but for its contribution to the manufacture of another. The demand by a firm for employees, land, buildings, machinery and raw materials originates only from the demand for the goods and services produced from these factors. The result of this dependence is that the intensity and elasticity of the demand for the resources is determined by the intensity and elasticity of the demand for the final product which those resources help to produce.

intermediate good A good such as a raw material or a component which is bought by a manufacturer as an input to the productive processes of the factory.

international comparative advantages The advantage that one country has over others in being able to change to the production a particular good with a lower sacrifice of alternative production than can other countries, and which determines the kind of production in which it specialises. This may arise out of its abundance of workers with special abilities, natural resources such as deposits of oil or minerals, fertile land, forests, a favourable climate, or the necessary amount and type of productive plant.

international division of labour Specialisation in production at the international level in which each country

International Monetary Fund A fund created by the United Nations in 1947 to assist the growth of international trade. It encourages international cooperation in the monetary field and the removal of foreign exchange restrictions. It supports the stabilisation of exchange rates and facilitates a multilateral payments system between member countries. It also provides member countries with short-term loans to allow them time to take the necessary measures to correct a mounting level of international debt. Also **IMF**.

international reserves A country's holdings of gold and the currencies of a few major countries (known as reserve currencies) that can be used to meet its needs for foreign currency to finance international transactions.

international trade The exchange of goods and services between one country and another. It takes place because of differences in costs of production between countries, and because it increases the economic welfare of each country by widening the range of goods and services available for consumption. Countries tend to specialise in the production for export of those goods and services in which they are relatively most efficient because of their natural and economic advantages. Countries devote home resources to exports because they can obtain more goods and services by international exchange than they would obtain from the same resources devoted to direct home production.

intervention Any form of government interference with market forces to achieve economic ends.

inventories Stocks of raw materials, components, work in progress or finished goods held by a firm in order to meet production needs or customers' orders promptly as they arise.

inventory investment The building up of inventories of finished goods by permitting production to exceed sales, or by the purchasing of more raw materials than can be absorbed by the current production level. The reverse process is 'inventory disinvestment'.

investment Investment expenditure.

investment demand Firms' desired or planned additions to their physical capital (plant and machinery) and to their inventories (stocks of raw materials or finished goods held for future production or sale).

investment demand schedule A table estimating for an economy the total amount of money which would be borrowed for industrial and commercial investment expenditure at each of a range of possible rates of interest.

investment expenditure Expenditure on capital goods such as plant, machinery and inventories, to replace worn-out or used-up stock and to increase the size of the stock.

investment goods Capital goods.

invisible earnings The net surplus balance on the invisible trade section of the balance of payments current account when invisible receipts from abroad exceed invisible payments to foreign countries.

invisible trade Payments to or from abroad for the provision of services (in distinction to merchandise). These services include such items as payments for transport by sea and air, salaries, profits, interest and dividends, premiums and commissions for banking and insurance, expenditure of tourists and other travellers.

iso-product curve A curve joining the points on a graph which plot the various combinations of two inputs (say, machinery and manpower) required to produce a given quantity of a particular product in the most efficient manner, that is, in each case with the minimum quantities of the two inputs.

isoquant An iso-product curve.

Jj

joint demand The situation when it is essential to use two or more raw materials or consumer goods in conjunction with one another. Such linked goods are generally demanded in similar proportions, a change in the quantity demanded for one producing a proportional change in the quantity demanded of the other.

joint products Goods that are unavoidably produced together by a given process.

joint supply When the processing of a raw material results in the production of two or more products. One may be regarded as the secondary by-product of the other, which is the main product. A change in the rate of output of one causes a similar change in the other. Any change in the conditions of demand for one product will influence the market for the other.

Ll

labour One of the traditional groupings of productive resources which together with land and capital formed the three factors of production. It is a collective name given to the totality of the many different types of physical and mental effort undertaken by individuals in contributing to the supply of goods and services.

labour cost per unit of output For any given level of output, the cost of the labour involved in producing that output divided by the quantity of the output.

labour force That part of the population which is employed or available for work. It comprises the population less mainly children of pre-school age, those in full-time education, retired people, persons fully employed in the home and persons incapable of working due to physical or mental disability.

labour force participation rate The proportion of the total labour force coming within a particular age, sex, industrial or other sub-group, expressed as a percentage of the proportion of the total population coming within the same sub-group.

labour input The total number of man-hours a firm employs.

labour-intensive industry An industry which employs in its productive processes a significantly higher ratio of labour input to capital input than the average ratio for industry as a whole.

labour market A collective term for the totality of formal and informal arrangements for bringing job vacancies to the attention of workers, of supplying workers for particular types of jobs, of hiring and dismissing workers and for determining their wages and conditions of employment.

labour mobility The ease or difficulty with which workers can move between jobs and areas. It concerns the willingess and ability of workers to change employers or occupations, or to move from one district to another, in response to differences in wages or job availability.

labour productivity Total output for a given period divided by the number of workers or the number of man-hours employed in the production of that output.

labour supply The total number of hours of work that the population of a country is willing to supply. This will depend on (1) the size of the total population, (2) the proportion of the total population available for employment which in turn will depend on such factors as the school-leaving age, the extent to which women are employed and the age of retirement, (3) the length of the working week and the amount of holidays taken.

labour turnover The number of workers who leave a firm or an industry in a year expressed as a percentage of the average number of workers employed during that year.

Laffer curve A curve joining the points on a graph which plot the relationship between tax revenue received by the state and the percentage tax rate imposed by the state. It shows that higher rates generate more revenue only up to a certain maximum rate. Increasing the tax rate further leads to a fall in total tax revenue because the disincentive effect outweighs the higher tax rates.

laissez-faire The principle of non-intervention of the government or other central authorities in the economic affairs of a country.

land One of the traditional groupings of productive resources which together with labour and capital formed the three factors of production. It is a collective term covering the space in which production may take place and also natural resources such as mineral deposits, fishing grounds, forests and fertile soil which are provided by the land (including the water).

lateral integration Horizontal integration.

law of diminishing marginal utility Diminishing marginal utility.

law of diminishing returns Diminishing marginal returns.

less developed countries Developing countries.

limit pricing The practice of existing firms in an industry to set the prices of their products at a level that will be just low enough for it not to be profitable for other firms to enter the industry.

limit to expansion As a firm expands, its marginal costs after a time tend to rise and its marginal revenue tends to fall. The limit to expansion will be at the point where marginal revenue and marginal cost are equal, since any expansion beyond that point will result in less profit.

liquid asset An asset which is in the form of currency or balances against which cheques can be drawn, or which can be quickly converted into such, with little loss.

liquidity The extent of the availability of currency and balances against which cheques can be drawn, and of assets readily convertible into such, to meet immediate demands for money.

liquidity preference The degree of preference for holding wealth in the form of currency or balances against which cheques can be drawn, instead of in interest-earning or dividend-paying securities.

liquidity ratio The proportion of the total assets of a bank or other financial intermediary which are held in the form of currency and other assets which can be quickly converted into cash.

long-run market supply

localisation of industry The tendency of the firms comprising certain industries to concentrate in a particular area.

location theory That section of economic theory which examines the reasons why firms or industries are sited in a particular place. It considers factors such as the transport costs arising from their proximity to sources of raw materials or to their markets.

long run A period long enough for a firm or an industry experiencing a long-term rise in the demand for its products, to expand its plant, machinery and other resources, so as to arrive at the most efficient combination of inputs to supply the additional output in the least expensive possible way.

long-run average cost The total cost of producing a given output divided by the number of units of output for a firm undergoing a continuous expansion of production under long-run conditions.

long-run cost schedule A table showing the lowest total, average and marginal costs of producing each of a series of output levels for a firm undergoing a continuous expansion of production under long-run conditions.

long-run industry supply The increase in the total supply of a product by an industry when the success of existing firms has stimulated new firms to enter the industry. The resulting increase in supply causes a readjustment of the market to a new lower equilibrium price. Such an increase takes place only after the interval of time required for new producers to enter the market.

long-run marginal costs The increase in total costs required to produce one more unit of output for a firm undergoing a continuous expansion of production under long-run conditions.

long-run market supply Long-run industry supply.

long-run total costs The total costs at each successive level of output for a firm undergoing a continuous expansion of production under long-run conditions.

Lorenz curve A line on a graph which plots the fraction of the national income (or some other economic aggregate) received by the poorest one per cent of households, by the poorest two per cent, by the poorest three per cent, and so on. When these points are joined, a perfectly even distribution would produce a straight line, but because distributions are inevitably uneven, a curve results. The greater the curvature of the curve, the greater the inequality.

luxury good A class of good on which a consumer spends a greater share of his income as his income rises. If his income rises by 1 per cent, the amount he purchases of a luxury good increases by more than 1 per cent. If his income falls by 1 per cent, the amount he purchases falls by more than 1 per cent.

Mm

macro-economics The study of the operation of an economy as a whole. It concerns relationships between broad economic totals and averages such as the total value of all the goods and services produced in a given period, the average level of prices of these goods and services, the total of everyone's income, the average level of wages, the total amount of money in use in the country, the total of consumers' spending and total saving.

maintaining capital intact Making good that part of the stock of a firm's, industry's or country's capital goods consumed in production. A certain amount of production must be allocated continuously to the replacement of worn-out or obsolete capital, otherwise total capital stock will decline.

Malthusian theory of population This maintained that population tended to increase in geometrical progression but that the food production necessary to sustain the increasing population could be increased only in arithmetical progression. Without personal restraint the point would be reached when the population would outstrip the means of feeding it and further population expansion would be checked by a counterbalancing increase in the death rate resulting from starvation and malnutrinion-related disease.

marginal analysis An analytical technique which studies the relationship between a very small increase or decrease in the quantity of one thing and the resulting small change in the quantity of a second thing which is influence by the first.

marginal cost The increase in a firm's total costs when one additional unit of output is produced. Fixed costs make no contribution to marginal cost because they do not change when output increases, and so marginal cost is entirely determined by the increase in variable cost.

marginal cost pricing A method of setting the price of a good or service by making it equal to the marginal cost of producing it. Its object is to set a fair price at the maximum level of production consistent with covering costs. It is achieved through variations in output. If the marginal cost is below the price, not enough of the good is being produced. If it is above the price, too much is being produced.

marginal costs, long-run Long-run marginal costs.

marginal costs, short-run Short-run marginal costs.

marginal firm A firm just capable of earning normal profits, that is, whose total profits are just high enough to compensate the the owners for the income that the money and physical assets they have invested in the firm might have earned in some alternative investment. If profits in the industry fall, the marginal firm will be the first to leave.

marginal physical product of a factor The extra units of output that result from employing one extra unit of that factor, the quantities of all other factors remaining constant.

marginal physical product of capital The extra units of output that result from employing one extra unit of capital, the quantities of all other factors remaining constant.

marginal physical product of labour The extra units of output that result from the employment of one extra man-hour of labour, the quantities of all other factors remaining constant.

marginal productivity theory That the demand for a factor of production is determined by the fact that an employer will employ more units of it up to the point where the cost of the last extra unit just equals its marginal physical product multiplied by the prevailing price per unit of that product. Thus the income of the factor (say, the wage of a worker or the rent of land) will tend to equal the marginal revenue product of the factor.

marginal propensity to consume The fraction of each extra pound of income that is spent instead of saved.

marginal propensity to save The fraction of each extra pound of income that is saved instead of spent.

marginal rate of substitution The amount of the reduced consumption of one commodity which is considered by the consumer to be compensated for by his consumption of one extra unit of another.

marginal revenue The change in a firm's total revenue when it increases its output by one unit.

marginal revenue product of a factor The addition to total revenue obtained by selling the marginal physical product of the factor.

marginal revenue product of labour The addition to total revenue obtained by selling the marginal physical product of labour.

marginal tax rate The percentage of each pound of extra income that is paid in tax.

marginal unit The last unit to be added to, or the first unit to be taken away from, any supply of a good or service.

marginal utility The additional satisfaction resulting from a one-unit increase in the consumption of a particular good.

marginal utility, law of diminishing Diminishing marginal utility.

marginal utility of money The extra utility which results from increasing by one unit the quantity of money an individual has. Since money is valued only because of its purchasing power, the marginal utility of money must derive from the marginal utilities of the goods on which it is spent. It is a common assumption that the marginal utility of money diminishes as the quantity of money possessed by an individual increases.

marginal wage cost The increase in total wage payments when the firm employs one more unit of labour.

market

market A situation where arrangements have been established for buyers and sellers of particular goods or services to be in sufficiently close contact with each other (without the necessity of actually meeting) for the goods or services in which they deal to tend to sell at the same price in all parts of the market. The market is not necessarily confined to any particular geographical location, and its dispersal may indeed be worldwide.

market clearing The movement of a market to the equilibrium position where the supply of a commodity matches the demand, resulting in all stocks being cleared.

market demand curve The line joining the points on a graph which plot the information contained in a market demand schedule.

market demand schedule A table giving for each of a range of prices, the total amount of a good or service that all the buyers in the market are willing to purchase at that price per week, month or year.

market disequilibrium A market situation when the quantity demanded and the quantity supplied of a good or service are not equal.

market economy An economy in which economic decisions and choices are made in a decentralised manner by numerous private individuals and firms operating through a market and price mechanism in which there is no government intervention.

market equilibrium The situation prevailing when at the ruling price the amount of goods or services being offered for sale is exactly matched by the amount consumers wish to buy.

market forces The influences of supply and demand which together determine the price at which a product is sold and the quantity which is traded.

market imperfections Features of a market structure which deviate from one or more of the conditions necessary for perfect competition.

market power The influence exercised by suppliers or buyers, individually or in groups, over the market price of the goods or services in which they deal.

market price The price prevailing in a market before the suppliers have had time to significantly increase or reduce their rate of output in response to that price. In these circumstances, the intensity of demand is the dominant influence on price.

market sector That sector of the economy concerned with the production of goods and services for which the cost of the production is recovered through their sale in the market. This is in distinction to the *non-market sector* where the money required to finance the production of the goods or services is not obtained through their market sale, but through public donation, local rates or taxation.

market share The percentage of total market sales in a given period that is attributable to one firm.

market structure A description of the main features of a market. These would include the number and size of the firms buying or selling the good or service involved, their geographical dispersal, their market shares, the extent of their vertical or horizontal integration, the ease with which new firms can enter the market, the extent of product differentiation, the stability and elasticity of demand and supply.

market supply The total supply of a good or service per week, month or year, provided by all the sellers in a market.

mass production Production carried out in large factories employing manufacturing techniques which involve the extensive use of specialised capital equipment and each worker having just a single operation to perform. The output is substantial and generally leads to a fall in prices if the manufacturers enjoy economies of scale as they expand.

mass unemployment The most serious type of unemployment associated with the trade cycle when households spend less and firms buy less new equipment. It is characterised by a general reduction in the demand for goods and services so that nearly all industries are affected at the same time. This causes a reduction in the demand for most or all types of labour.

maximisation of profits An assumption of economic theory that producers aim at adjusting their production techniques and level of output to that which will give them the greatest profit.

medium of exchange A means of overcoming the direct good-for- good exchange problems of the barter system. It is an intermediary which can be given to buy goods and will be readily accepted when goods are sold, in the confidence that it can be retained without losing its value and then re-used to buy further goods. Today, money performs this function, but in the past other objects have served this purpose.

merit goods and services Those which the state believes are unquestionably desirable in the interests of public welfare and whose consumption should be encouraged or made compulsory. Such goods and services may be provided free or at greatly subsidised prices. Examples are the services for health, education, social welfare, employment and the arts.

microeconomics That branch of economics which studies the causes, effects and interactions of economic decisions made by individuals, households, firms and industries. It examines consumers' decisions on what to buy, firms' decisions on what to produce, and the determination of relative wages and prices operating in particular markets or industries. This is in distinction to *macroeconomics* which concerns totals for the economy as a whole such as national income, national output, the general level of prices or of unemployment.

mixed economy An economy in which resources are allocated partly through the decisions of private individuals and privately-owned business enterprises and partly through

model

the decisions of the government and state-owned enterprises. The absolute extremes of complete direction from the centre and complete freedom from government interference are not found in reality. In practice, all economies are mixed economies. The difference between nations is in the degree of centralised control. In some the influence of the government is substantially less than others.

mobility of capital Industrial and commercial buildings are capable of alternative uses, but most plant and machinery is highly specific to a single product. In the long run, however, plant and machinery wears out and can then be replaced with new types which are suited to changed demand.

mobility of factors of production The ease with which land, buildings, capital equipment and workers may be transferred occupationally or geographically from one employment to another. Most factors of production are not completely specific to one line of production, and the less specific they are, the greater is their mobility.

mobility of labour This has two aspects. (1) Occupational mobility, that is, the ease with which workers can be transferred from one type of work to another. (2) Geographical mobility, that is, the willingness and ability of workers to move from districts where work is difficult to obtain to those where there is a greater employment opportunity.

mobility of land Obviously land is not mobile in the geographical sense, but it can be put to alternative uses, that is, it has occupational mobility. It can, for example, be employed as farmland or for forestry, or it can be built upon.

model A theory which tries to explain how an economic phenomenon (such as a change in the price of a commodity) has come about. The complex real-world situation will be affected by a number of changing and inter-related factors. In the analysis of such situations, it is necessary for purposes of clarity to identify the most important factors and to assume that the rest remain unchanged. Although this may mean that the model is to some extent unrealistic, it may still give far more insight into a problem, and far more predictive ability, than would a less abstract approach which tried to take everything into account.

monetarism Monetarist theory.

monetarist theory This stresses the role of the quantity of money and credit and the rate of interest in influencing economic activity. It emphasises the effectiveness of monetary rather than fiscal policy to change national income and the inflation rate, and the ineffectiveness of monetary and fiscal policies designed to change the level of employment.

monetarists Those who believe that monetary policy is the most important means available to a government for influencing the level of economic activity.

monetary base The total monetary liability of the central government, this being composed of the notes and coin it has issued for public use plus its liabilities to the banking system in the form of reserves they hold at the central bank. This is the determinant of a country's money supply which, through the mutiplier effect of the bank reserve/deposit ratio, is a multiple of the money base.

monetary policy Government policy that determines the way in which the government finances its budget deficit or uses a budget surplus. Its objective is to serve national economic goals such as the control of inflation or reduction in the level of unemployment. It involves decisions on the level of borrowing and changes in the money supply and the cost and availability of credit. To this end it regulates the activities of banks and other financial institutions.

money Anything that is generally accepted not for itself but only as a means of payment for goods and services and for settling debts. The functions of money are as a medium of exchange, a store of value and a unit of account.

money as a medium of exchange It provides a means of overcoming the direct good-for-good exchange problems of the barter system. It is an intermediary which can be given to buy goods and will be readily accepted when goods are sold in the confidence that it can be re-used to buy further goods.

money as a store of value It provides a means of holding one's assets in a form in which they can be easily exchanged for other assets in the future. People may not wish to spend all their money immediately but may wish to save it for future spending. They hold money as long as they are confident that others will accept it when they want to spend it and that there will not be any deterioration in its value in the meantime.

money as a unit of account It provides a means of simplifying the measurement and comparison of wealth by enabling the value of commodities, debts, assets and all forms of payment to be quoted and calculated in the same unit.

money demand The need of individuals and firms to have readily available cash in order to meet everyday predictable spending requirements, unforeseen contingency payments and temporary excesses of payments over receipts.

money holding Keeping savings as cash in hand or in an account against which cheques can be issued, as distinct from investing it in various kinds of interest-earning or dividend-paying securities.

money illusion The experience of a person who, having received a wage rise, believes that he is better off and adjusts his spending pattern on the basis of his increased money wage without regard to the fact that due to general price rises his real wage has not risen at the same rate as his money wage.

money supply The amount of money which exists in an economy at a given time. The essence of money is that it be generally accepted as a means of payment. Thus notes and coins are clearly part of the money supply. In addition, current accounts at banks are through the use of cheques also used to settle debts and so are also part of the money supply. Beyond this there are various definitions as to what other categories of liquid assets should be included. Those for Britain are given below, varying with the degree of liquidity and starting with M0 as the most liquid.

money supply—M0 (M-nought) This comprises the notes and coins in circulation and the deposits which the banks voluntarily keep at the Bank of England (as distinct from the statutory cash ratio deposits). It is regarded as the monetary base.

money supply—M1 This comprises the notes and coins in circulation and the deposits which the banks voluntarily keep at the Bank of England (as distinct from the statutory cash ratio deposits) plus sterling current accounts at banks which, through the use of cheques, are also used to settle debts.

money supply—M2 M1 plus deposit accounts with banks, building societies and National Savings accounts from which the money can be withdrawn without notice. Deposit accounts are strictly speaking not capable of being used as money, but the scope for easy withdrawals from them, or transfers between deposit and current accounts, places them within this broader definition of the money supply. It has however ceased to be used in official UK money statistics.

money supply—M3 (sterling M3) M1 plus deposit accounts with banks, building societies and National Savings accounts from which the money can be withdrawn without notice, plus accounts of households and privately owned firms in sterling (pounds) from which withdrawals require a period of notice, plus the bank accounts in sterling of the government, local authorities and other public authorities.

money supply—M3 Sterling M3 plus bank deposits in foreign currencies held by British residents.

money supply—PSL1 (private sector liquidity) The private sector's share of sterling M3 plus the private sector's holdings of treasury bills, deposits with local authorities and certificates of tax deposits which companies buy to set aside for future tax liabilities.

money supply—PSL2 The first two components of PSL1 plus the private sector's savings deposits, shares and other securities.

money veil   The money illusion.

monopolistic competition   A market structure in which competition exists between many sellers of goods which are close but not perfect substitutes for one another. Products are differentiated by means of distinctive brand names, variations in preparation and presentation, and by advertising. Because each sells a slightly different good, each seller has a limited ability to affect the price at which he sells. New firms can enter the market freely.

monopoly   The theoretical concept of a market structure in which a single firm controls the entire production and sale of a good or service for which there is no close substitute, new firms being unable to enter the market. Absolute monopoly is rare in real life because there are few goods or services for which there is not some sort of substitute. In practice the term is used of any firm or combination of firms that produces so large a proportion of the total output that it can raise price by restricting output. Even so, a monopolist must take account of consumers' demand. He can either fix his price and let demand determine his output, or fix his output and let demand determine the price, but he cannot do both of these things.

monopoly, discriminating   Discriminating monopoly.

monopoly power   The ability of a trading organisation to exercise some measure of control over the price or the level of supply of the good or service in which it deals.

monopsony   A market structure where there is only one buyer of a good or service or where there is only one major employer of a factor of production.

multilateral trade   International trade between more than two countries where the trade between any two may not necessarily balance, but the total exports of any one to all the others will tend to balance its total imports from them.

multiplier   The ratio of the change in national income to the change in the level of investment or consumer spending that causes the income change, once the total effect has had time to work itself through the economic system. It is equal to 1 divided by the marginal propensity to save. Thus the greater the marginal propensity to save, the smaller the multiplier.

multiplier effect The sequence of events that follows an injection into the circular flow of national income. An investment or consumer spending increase gives extra income in the form of wages, rent, profit, etc. to those working in the industries involved. They will save some of the extra income and spend the rest. This spending will in its turn cause increased output, employment and a further round of extra income. Part of this will be saved and part spent. This process will repeat itself, its effect diminishing with each round because part of the income is saved instead of being passed on in spending. When this process has worked itself out, the total extra income created will be several times greater than the value of the originating injection.

Nn

national debt The debt accumulated over many years by the central government. It has risen whenever the government's total revenues have failed to finance their total spending, and it has been necessary for them to resort to borrowing. This has been done mostly through the issue of interest-bearing securities promising to repay the amounts borrowed to their holders at a specified future date.

national economic goals The major objectives pursued by governments to improve the material wellbeing of their countries. They include a high and stable level of employment, a satisfactory rate of economic growth, an equitable distribution of national income, reasonable price stability, and equilibrium in the the country's international balance of payments.

national income The total amount earned as wages, rent, interest, dividends, profit, etc. by the individuals who contributed to the production of a country's national product of goods and services. One method of calculating the value of the national product is to add together all these incomes.

national incomes policy A policy of restraint in relation to increases in personal incomes with the object of slowing down inflationary trends. The object is to keep increases in personal incomes broadly in line with increases in the productivity of industry.

national real output Full employment national income.

national product The money value of all the goods and services produced in an economy in a given year. Since the amounts paid for the goods and services result in the incomes in the form of wages, rent, interest, dividends, profit, etc. of the individuals who contributed to their production, one method of calculating the national product is to add together all these incomes to give the national income. Since the total spending on the goods and services is just another way of expressing their sales value, a further method of calculating the national product is to estimate the total spending of individuals and public authorities in consuming it. Finally it can be calculated by adding up the addition to the value of the unfinished outputs as they pass through each stage of production to arrive at the final value of the finished consumer goods and services.

nationalisation A policy of state ownership and control of an entire industry or a single firm. It may be undertaken on grounds of ideology as the most efficient and fair method of organising economic activities, to control natural monopolies, or to keep in existence firms who would otherwise have closed down.

nationalised industry One which produces and markets goods and services direct to consumers or other producers, but is owned and controlled by the state.

natural monopoly An industry in which there would be an unavoidable need for all competing firms to rapidly expand due to the incentive of steeply falling average costs until eventually competition would give way to market domination by a single firm. This firm would be able to produce the total output of the industry at a lower average cost than any greater number of firms. The situation arises when it is possible to produce a good or service only in high-cost complex plants involving the installation and maintenance of a large amount of equipment. Water, gas or electricity supply fall within this category.

natural oligopoly An industry in which competing firms have expanded due to the incentive of falling long-run costs and in which competition has quickly given way to market domination by a few large producers.

natural protection A protection against competition that is derived purely from the nature of the product or the geographical position of the producer, and without the necessity to take special measures. Bulky or non-durable products involve relatively high transport costs and hence there is a need for the producer to be physically close to the market. In consequence it is costly for potential competitors to enter the market with supplies from other regions. The immediacy or convenience of the proximity of a supplier to his customers may protect him from their loss to rival firms.

natural rate of unemployment A level of unemployment considered to be unavoidable even in times of national prosperity. It is accounted for by the inevitable interim short-term unemployment of those in process of changing jobs.

natural resources Productive resources which are available to a country because of its geographical position and geological structure. They include oil, coal and metal ore deposits, forests, fertile soil, rivers and lakes, rainfall, sunshine, etc.

near money Amounts lodged in bank deposit accounts or in building societies which, although in this form they cannot be used to make payments, can nevertheless be quickly and easily converted into cash or a cheque.

necessity good That type of good on which a household spends a smaller proportion of its income as its income increases, and on which it spends a higher proportion of its income as its income falls. If a household's income increases by one per cent, it buys more of all necessities, but it increases its consumption of each necessity by less than one per cent. If the household's income falls by one per cent, it reduces its demand for necessities by less than one per cent. It is thus a good with an income elasticity of demand of less than 1.

negative income tax A government payment to individuals whose income falls below a prescribed level in order to bring them up to that level.

negative investment Disinvestment.

negative real growth This occurs when, after having taken into account the effect of inflation on price levels, there is a contraction in the value of the gross national product of a country from one year to another.

negative real interest rate An interest rate which is lower than the rate of inflation. Thus a lender or an investor becomes worse off in real terms because the monetary appreciation of the sum loaned or invested does not keep pace with the rate of inflation.

net capital formation The amount of the increase in a firm's, an industry's or the country's stock of buildings, plant, machinery and other equipment, after having provided for the replacement of worn-out and obsolete stock. This equals the excess of total spending on these items over the amount required to make good depreciation.

net domestic product at factor cost The value of the nation's total output of goods and services in one year, adjusted for the price effect of indirect taxes and subsidies, and after deducting the cost of replacing worn-out productive assets such as buildings, plant and equipment. It may be negative if not enough expenditure is made to replace depreciation fully.

net exports For a given period, the excess of the total value of goods and services sold abroad by a country over the total value of the goods and services it has bought from abroad.

net investment Net capital formation.

net national product at factor cost The net domestic product at factor cost plus the incomes of domestic residents received from abroad as salaries, dividends or interest, minus similar payments made to residents of other countries.

net present value of an investmnt The difference between the cost of purchasing a new building, machine or other item of equipment for use in a business, and the sum of money calculated as being equal to the present value of the future

non-price competition

flow of income to which it is estimated that the investment will give rise.

net property income from abroad The difference between incomes of home residents received from abroad as dividends, profits or interest from assets held overseas, and similar payments made to residents of other countries on assets they hold in the home country.

nominal price Price measured in monetary terms.

nominal wages Earnings measured in terms of their current value in units of money. This is to be compared with real wages which are nominal wages adjusted for changes in the general price level over time and which compare wages in terms of the goods and services they will buy.

non-luxury good A necessity good.

non-market sector That sector of the economy concerned with the production of goods and services for which the money required to finance production is not obtained through their sale in the market, but through public donation, local rates or taxation.

non-monetary advantages The desirable aspects of some types of work that, by increasing the desirability of the occupations, may have some compensating effect on the occupational wage rates. The working environment may be pleasant, the work itself may be interesting or carry social status or be very secure, or the worker may be given a lot of independence.

non-price competition A method of trying to increase a firm's share of a market while leaving the list prices of the products unchanged. The firm seeks to attract new customers and retain existing customers through self-identifying labelling, attractive packaging, advertising, a reputation for quality, after-sales services, the introduction of new brands, bonuses, gifts, etc.

non-renewable resource One such as a mineral deposit of which there is a fixed irreplaceable amount and hence which will be eventually exhausted.

non-specific factors of production Factors that are not specialised and so can more easily be moved to alternative uses. Examples are unskilled labour, some unprocessed raw materials, and land which is capable of being used for grazing, agriculture, building or recreation.

normal good A good for which demand increases when income rises and for which demand decreases when income falls, that is, for which the income elasticity of demand is positive.

normal price The equilibrium price.

normal profit That part of a firm's total profits that represents the compensation to the owners for the alternative income they might have made from the money or their own land, buildings or other assets that they have invested in the firm. This level of profit is necessary if capital is to be attracted to or retained in that line of production, otherwise it could be more profitably invested elswhere. It represents the opportunity cost of the owners' invested resources which equals the greatest income that could be received from their alternative use.

normal unemployment rate The natural rate of unemployment.

Oo

obsolescence A reduction in the useful life of a capital good or consumer durable good through economic or technological change as distinct from physical deterioration in use. Due to technological advance, machinery and equipment may become obsolete long before the termination of its physical life. The question then arises as to whether the cost of replacing it would be more than offset by benefits arising from the increased efficiency of the new plant. If so, it has reached the end of its economic life, that is, it has become obsolete and ought to be replaced by more efficient capital.

occupational wage differentials The extent of the difference between the average wage of the workers in any one of a group of occupations and the average wages being paid in each of the remainder.

oligopoly A market structure in which a few large firms produce all or most of the output of a particular industry, and in which there is a high degree of interdependence among the decisions of the firms. In planning any sales strategy, each firm is strong enough to influence the market but not strong enough to disregard the possible reactions of its competitors. The entry of new firms may be restricted by the actions of firms already supplying the market. There is a tendency in such markets for the basis of competition to shift from price to non-price matters such as quality, advertising and after-sales services.

oligopsony The counterpart of oligopoly. A market situation in which a few large buyers purchase all or most of the output of a particular industry.

on costs Variable costs.

open economy One which is involved in overseas trade.

open market operations The purchase or sale of securities by the central bank with the monetary policy objectives of influencing the volume of credit and the money supply. It does this by increasing or decreasing the reserves held by the banking system at the central bank. Selling securities to the banks will contract their reserves and compel a reduction in bank loans. It will also reduce the level of bank deposits and hence the money supply. Buying securities will have the reverse effect.

operating costs Variable costs.

operating profit The amount in a given period by which a firm's income from selling its goods or services exceeds its expenses of producing them. This amount will be distributed in the form of interest or dividends or retained as undistributed profits for the self-financing of the future expansion of the firm.

opportunity cost The real cost of acquiring any item, which is the alternative that has to be forgone in order to do so. Because resources are limited, the choice of one thing involves doing without something else.

opportunity cost—firm A firm's opportunity cost of producing good X, measured in units of good Y, is the reduction in its production of good Y when it increases his production of good X by one unit.

opportunity cost—household A household's opportunity cost of good X measured in terms of good Y is the the number of units of good Y that the household has to give up in order to buy one more unit of good X.

opportunity cost—worker The opportunity cost of a worker in remaining in a particular employment is the amount that he could earn in his highest-paying alternative employment.

opportunity cost of holding money The amount of income that is sacrificed by holding assets in the form of money rather than by investing them in interest-earning or dividend-paying securities.

optimisation The assumption in economic analysis that the consumer will spend his disposable income in such a way as to maximise his total utility or satisfaction, and also that the producer will plan production so as to maximise his profits and minimise his costs.

optimum The most satisfactory situation giving the best possible balance of advantages against disadvantages.

optimum firm A firm in a position of maximum efficiency in which the costs of production per unit of output are at a minimum. Expansion up to this size is accompanied by falling average costs and increasing returns as a result of economies of scale. Beyond this point, costs begin to rise and diminishing returns set in.

optimum population The population of a country may be too large or too small in proportion to the country's other factors of production. Given the situation of its natural and physical resources, there is a theoretical best population which provides that number of workers which, when combined with the other factors of production, yields the maximum output.

origin The point on a demand schedule corresponding to the minimum amount of a commodity that must be acquired before it can be used effectively. If the quantity acquired is below this point, it is too small to be of effective use and therefore any additional amount will have a greater utility than the previous unit. Successive increments will show increasing utility up to the origin, and decreasing utility beyond the origin.

output The quantity of goods or services produced by a firm, industry or country in a given period of time.

output gap The difference between a country's actual output of goods and services and the potential output that could be produced if there were full employment. It thus measures the amount of output lost through unemployment.

overheads Fixed costs.

overpopulation The situation of a country when the contribution of additional people applying given techniques to a given quantity of productive resources would lower the per capita national product. Once output does not grow in proportion to additional population, output per person must fall.

overvalued currency One whose exchange rate is fixed above the rate at which it would settle if the forces of the free international currency market were allowed to operate.

Pp

paradox of thrift   The apparent contradiction that, in hard times of mass unemployment and idle workplaces, the more the population practises the morally commendable principle of thrift, the lower becomes the level of national output, employment and industrial and commercial activity. The reduced consumption decreases the level of total demand which in its turn reduces the level of output and factor employment.

paradox of value   The apparent enigma as to why a good such as water, which is essential to life, has a low price compared with that of non-essential luxuries such as diamonds.

partial equilibrium analysis   The examination of the factors which determine the equilibrium position for a small sector of the economy such as a single consumer, a single firm or a market for a particular commodity, assuming that prices in all other sectors remain unchanged.

per capita   Per head.

per capita gross national product   The gross national product of a country for a particular year divided by the country's population in that year. It is the value per person, including children and others not working, of the goods and services produced in that year.

per capita income   The total income of a particular social or economic group divided by the number of people in the group.

perfect competition   The relationship between buyers and sellers that exists in the theoretical concept of a perfectly competitive market. The necessary conditions are (1) many sellers and buyers (2) homogeneous goods (3) equal treatment of buyers (4) no restriction on entry of new sellers and buyers (5) perfect information (6) unrestricted movement of the commodity. These conditions are rarely all present in real-life situations, but they are a starting point for analysing to what extent reality departs from this theoretical norm.

perfect competition—equal treatment of buyers One of the conditions required for a perfectly competitive market whereby all buyers are identical from the point of view of the suppliers. There is no preferential treatment of favoured buyers, the suppliers simply selling to the highest bidder.

perfect competition—homogeneous goods One of the conditions required for a perfectly competitive market whereby the goods produced by all firms are so similar that customers have no preference for the products of any particular seller. There is no reason why they would buy from anyone but the cheapest seller. Since anyone who charges more than this minimum must expect to sell nothing, every seller must sell at the same price.

perfect competition—many sellers and buyers One of the conditions required for a perfectly competitive market whereby there are so many sellers and buyers that their individual supply or demand is only a small fraction of the total. They accept the prevailing market price, being aware that they are unable to influence it by increasing or curtailing their individual supplies or purchases, these being too small to influence total demand or supply. Further, buyers and sellers do not collaborate to affect prices.

perfect competition—perfect information One of the conditions required for a perfectly competitive market whereby buyers and sellers are promptly and continuously aware of what is happening in all parts of the market. Every buyer knows which seller charges the lowest price, and every seller knows which buyer will pay the highest price, so that demand in one part of the market immediately affects prices in all other parts of the market.

perfect competition—unrestricted entry One of the conditions required for a perfectly competitive market whereby new buyers and sellers face no barrier to entry to the market, being able on entry to trade on exactly the same terms as existing buyers and sellers.

perfect competition—unrestricted movement One of the conditions required for a perfectly competitive market whereby there is an absence of any type of restriction on the transferability of the commodity from one part of the market to another.

perfect elasticity of demand The state of demand when buyers are prepared to buy all they can at a particular price but will buy nothing if the price rises even slightly beyond this point.

perfect elasticity of supply The state of supply when sellers are prepared to sell all they can at a given price but will sell nothing if the price falls even slightly below this point.

perfect inelasticity The state of demand or supply when the quantity demanded or supplied does not change as the price changes.

perfect information Perfect competition—perfect information.

perfect market A market structure which satisfies all the conditions of perfect competition.

personal disposable income The net income, after tax or other deductions from the gross income, received by an individual and available to him either for spending or saving.

personal income The gross income, before tax or other deductions, received by an individual from whatever source. It may be received as wages, salary, interest, dividends, fees, rent, drawings from business funds, pension or social security benefit.

personal saving The part of an individual's disposable income which is not spent but is used to add to his wealth.

personal saving rate Personal saving expressed as a percentage of personal disposable income.

physical capital The material assets which a firm uses in conjunction with its labour force to produce goods and services. They consist of (1) fixed capital, which includes durable goods such as industrial and commercial buildings, plant, machinery and equipment, means of communication and transport, or (2) floating or circulating capital, which includes rapidly rotating stocks of raw materials, fuels, components, semi-finished goods and unsold goods.

planned economy A centrally-controlled economy.

plant capacity The output of a firm when it is operating at minimum short-run average total cost.

point elasticity of demand The calculation of the change in the quantity demanded of a commodity in response to a price change, when the change in price is very small. The two points on the demand curve which represent demand before and after the change in price, are so close together that they virtually form a single point.

population trap A situation where the population of a country is growing at a higher rate than the rate of expansion in the country's output of goods and services. The result is a continuing fall in real income per head of the population.

positive economics That section of economics which attempts to explain objectively how an economy 'does' work. This is to be compared with *normative* economics which deals with ethical judgements regarding how the economy 'ought' to work in the interests of social welfare or justice.

potential national output Full employment national income.

poverty trap The reduction or removal of a household's incentive to earn more when doing so will cause it to lose income-related social security benefits and possibly to begin to pay income tax. In extreme cases, a household's total

price change effect

income may fall because the sum of the loss of benefits and increased tax payments exceeds the extra income from employment.

predatory pricing Temporarily sacrificing profits in order to reduce prices to below-cost levels for a period long enough to cause competitors to lose money and leave the industry.

precautionary demand for money A reason for holding money additional to that required for anticipated day-to-day spending. It arises out of the possibility of unforeseen needs for expenditure which otherwise might have to be financed by selling securities or other assets at penalty costs or at a time when unfavourable market conditions might result in a loss.

present value The value now of a sum of money payable at a future date. It is equivalent to the sum which if invested now at the prevailing rate of interest would produce the given sum at the future date. It is calculated by dividing the future sum by 100 plus this rate of interest. This is called 'discounting' and can also be done for a future flow of income to find its present value.

price The quantity of money which must be given in exchange for one unit of a good or service. In respect of human services the equivalent terms 'wage' 'salary' 'commission' or 'fee' are used. The price of borrowing money is called 'interest' and the price of hiring land, premises or equipment is called 'rent'.

price ceiling The maximum amount that sellers are legally allowed to charge for a specified good or service in accordance with rules imposed by the government.

price change effect The change in the demand for a good or service caused by a change in its price. It results from the interaction of two effects, the income effect and the substitution effect. An increase in the price of a good has an income effect because the real income of the consumer is reduced, and this will cause him to reshuffle his spending pattern on all goods and services in the light of their new

price controls

relative prices. The substitution effect arises because the consumer will consider buying a substitute in place of the higher-priced good.

price controls Government imposed restrictions that regulate or forbid price rises in all or specified goods and services in a situation of inflation.

price discrimination The charging by a supplier of different prices to different groups of customers for the same goods or services, for reasons not associated with differences in costs. It enables the supplier to make a higher profit by adjusting his prices to the different elasticities of demand prevailing in the various groups of customers.

price discrimination—enabling conditions For price discrimination to work (1) it must be possible to prevent resale of goods between customers, or such resale must be impracticable for customers to arrange (2) the seller must be able to control the amount of a product that is offered to a particular customer (3) the customers must be members of separate markets with different elasticities of demand in each market.

price elasticity of demand A measure of the degree of responsiveness of the quantity demanded of a good to a change in its price. It is measured by dividing the percentage change in quantity demanded by the percentage price change. If this gives a result larger than 1, demand is said to be elastic, that is, a rise or fall in price produces a more than proportionate change in the amount demanded. If it is less than 1, demand is said to be inelastic, that is, there is a less than proportionate change in the amount demanded in response to a price change.

price elasticity of supply A measure of the degree of responsiveness of the quantity supplied of a good to a change in its price. It is measured by dividing the percentage change in quantity supplied by the percentage price change. If this gives a result larger than 1, supply is said to be elastic, that is, a rise or fall in price produces a more than proportionate change in the amount supplied. If it is less than 1, supply is said to be inelastic, that is, there is a less than proportionate change in the amount supplied in response to a price change.

price increase anticipation In certain circumstances a rise in price may cause consumers to buy more of a commodity because they fear further price rises and wish to secure a stock of the commodity before these take place or because they speculate on selling the commodity at a profit.

price index number A number which gives the the ratio of the cost of purchasing a particular selection of commodities in a given year to the cost of purchasing the same selection in a base year for which the base number is set at 100. For example, an index number of 120 indicates a percentage increase in prices of 20 per cent over those ruling in the base year.

price index of exports (imports) This measures the change in the aggregate value of a representative selection of exports (imports) as compared with their corresponding values in a base year.

price leader A firm that by changing the prices of its products gives the signal to the other firms in the industry to change their prices.

price level The average level of the money prices for a particular range of commodities or for all commodities.

price makers A seller or a buyer whose share of the market is sufficiently large to enable him to control to his advantage the price at which he buys or sells.

price mechanism The process whereby the free movement of prices in unrestricted markets brings supply into balance with demand. If there is a situation of undersupply, price will rise. In response to a rising price, buyers reduce the quantities they wish to buy, and sellers increase the quantities they wish to sell. There may be over-reaction by suppliers, and the situation may change to one of oversupply. Price will now fall causing supply to be reduced and purchases to

price setters

increase. Following such fluctuations, the equilibrium price is eventually reached at which supply is equal to demand.

price setters   Price makers.

price stabilisation   The reduction in the fluctuations which would normally occur in the price of a commodity being bought and sold under volatile free market conditions. Schemes with this objective fix an estimated equilibrium price at which a central agency is prepared to buy or sell the commodity, and store any surplus for future sale in the event of shifts in supply and demand that result in an shortages.

price system   A price mechanism.

price taker   A buyer or a seller whose requirements or output is small relative to the size of the market and who cannot therefore influence the market price. He can only make a decision whether to buy or sell at the prevailing market price.

price theory   That section of economics concerned with analysing the ways in which prices are determined in a free market economy, and the role they play in solving the problems of resource allocation.

prices and incomes policy   Government policy that attempts to control the inflation rate by restraining increases in prices, money wages, and other incomes.

primary industry   That sector of industry concerned with the extraction of the raw materials required by the manufacturing sector. It includes mining, quarrying, agriculture, forestry and fishing.

prime costs   Costs that can be reduced or avoided if the firm is compelled by poor trade to work short-time for a lengthy period, or if it ceases to produce but nevertheless remains open for business. These include all variable costs like labour, power and raw materials, together with certain administration costs that arise only out of high capacity production.

private costs and benefits The monetary costs and incomes arising exclusively to the firm that carries out a productive activity and which are recorded in its accounts. They are to be distinguished from the social costs and benefits which include both the private costs and benefits and the costs and benefits caused by the external effects of the productive activities such as pollution, noise, environmental depreciation or time saved due to improved transport facilities.

private enterprise Economic activity in which the productive resources are owned by private persons, individually or jointly or in association, and in which production is undertaken for private profit. This is in distinction to *public enterprise* undertaken by local and central government and other public agencies.

private goods and services Those that can be consumed or used by only a single person. This implies that his consumption of the good or service reduces the quantity of it that can be enjoyed by others.

private sector All commercial and industrial firms in the economy which are not a part of, or agencies for, central or local government.

private sector balance The difference between households' total savings and total investment by privately owned firms.

privatisation (1) The selling back by the Government into private ownership of all or a part of a firm or an industry that had previously been nationalised. (2) The granting of permission by the Government to firms in the private sector to compete with a nationalised organisation in the provision of a service for which the latter had previously been the sole supplier.

producer goods Capital goods.

producers' indifference curve An iso-product curve.

producers' surplus The excess of the total earnings of a firm over the minimum that would have to be paid to persuade it to continue to supply the same quantity of a commodity. Such a minimum payment would need to cover only its total cost of production of the quantity involved.

product differentiation The creation of real or imagined differences in essentially the same type of product by means of branding, packaging, advertising, quality variation, design variation, etc. The purpose is to distinguish the product from those of competitors and build up its consumer loyalty.

production The process of converting raw materials into the goods and services required by the private individual, by private firms and by the public authorities, and also of conveying the goods to their ultimate customers. It thus includes the industrial activities of extraction, manufacturing and construction, and the commercial activities of retail and wholesale distribution together with the supporting services of banking, insurance, transport, communication, warehousing.

production possibility curve A curve joining the points on a graph which plot the technically feasible combinations of goods X and Y that can be made with a given amount of productive resources. It shows for each level of the output of one good the maximum amount of the other good that can be produced. Output of good X can be increased only at the expense of a reduction in the output of good Y and the transfer of the resources thus saved into the production of X.

production theory The branch of economics concerned with analysing the determinants of the firm's choice of quantities of inputs, the prices of the inputs and the level of output desired. The theory is based on the hypothesis that the firm will wish to use that set of quantities of the inputs which minimises the cost of producing a given output.

production time lag The time interval between a decision to undertake production and the beginning of the outflow of

production transformation curve A production possibility curve.

productive resources The inputs such as manpower, factory buildings, machinery, vehicles, raw materials that a firm requires in order to produce a good or service.

productivity Total output divided by the number of units of a particular input employed to produce that output. The motive for increasing productivity is to produce more goods at a lower cost per unit of output. For any given resource (say manpower) it is expressed as the number of units of output (say tons of steel) per unit of input (man-hours).

products Goods and services.

profit margin The percentage of the price of an article or a service that represents the producer's profit.

profit maximisation The assumption made in the theory of the firm that all its actions will be governed by the objective of achieving the highest possible profit.

profit-maximising output Profits are maximised by expanding output while the marginal revenue of each additional unit of output is greater than the maginal cost incurred in producing it. Expansion will cease at the level of output at which marginal revenue equals marginal cost. Beyond this point, the rising marginal cost would begin to exceed marginal revenue and thus involve a loss.

progressive taxation A system of taxation which increases the proportion of income taken in tax as income increases.

property income Income derived from the ownership of assets such as from renting land, buildings or equipment, from interest on money loaned, or from dividends on shares.

proportional taxation A system of taxation which takes the same proportion of income as tax at all income levels.

protection The imposition by the state of tariffs or quotas to restrict the inflow of imports. Such action may be undertaken because of the need to encourage self-sufficiency, to protect a growing industry, to retaliate to similar action on the part of other countries, or to combat the threat of unemployment.

PSBR Public sector borrowing requirement.

public authorities A collective term covering the central government, the local authorities and the nationalised industries that together make up the public sector.

public debt The debt accumulated over many years by the central government, the local authorities and the nationalised industries. It has risen whenever their total revenues have failed to finance their total spending, and it has been necessary for them to resort to borrowing.

public debt ratio A nation's public debt expressed as a ratio of its gross national product.

public enterprise Economic activity in a mixed economy carried out by the central government, the local authorities and the nationalised industries, as distinct from that carried out by private individuals and firms.

public expenditure Spending by the central government, the local authorities and the nationalised industries as distinct from spending by private individuals and firms. It comprises (1) spending on goods and services (2) the salaries of public employees (3) all forms of grants and social security transfer payments (4) interest on the public debt (5) capital expenditure.

public finance A branch of economics which analyses the effects of central government and local authority income and expenditure activities on the economic situation of individuals and firms and on the economy as a whole.

public goods and services Those such as national defence or an improved street lighting scheme which can only be provided communally without the possibility of excluding anyone. No private firm could sell such a provision because, due to its communal nature, it would be impossible to provide for one individual and withhold from another who refused to pay. The provision is therefore made by public authorities, payment by all being compelled through powers of taxation or rating.

public sector That section of the economy collectively owned by the public at large at national, regional or district level, as distinct from that in private ownership. It includes the central government, the local authorities and the nationalised industries.

public sector borrowing requirement The amount by which the the total revenue of the central government, the local authorities and the nationalised industries fails to finance their total spending and lending, and which will accordingly need to be financed by borrowing. Also PSBR.

pump priming Deficit financing.

purchasing power of money Money regarded from the viewpoint of the amount of goods and services that can be bought with a standard unit of currency. When the general price level of goods rises, the purchasing power of money falls because the pound, dollar or franc will buy fewer goods.

purchasing power parity theory A theory, not supported by practical experience, which suggests that the exchange rate between one currency and another will depend upon the relative price levels in the different countries. If, for example, the exchange rate of French francs for the British pound rose from 10 to 12, this would imply a relative increase of prices in France of 20 per cent, or alternatively a corresponding fall in the domestic purchasing power of French currency. Thus the rise in the price level will be offset by a fall of the exchange rate so that the price of the country's exports will tend to remain the same.

pure competition Perfect competition.

pure monopoly Absolute monopoly.

pure profit Supernormal profit.

Qq

quantity demanded The number of units of a commodity that a buyer is willing and able to buy at a given price.

quantity of money Money supply.

quantity supplied The number of units of a commodity that a supplier is willing to sell at a given price.

quantity theory of money A theory concerning the relationship between changes in the quantity of money in circulation in an economy and rises and falls in the general price level. The theory is based on the equation $MV = PT$ where M is the amount of money in circulation, V is the velocity of circulation of that money, P is the general price level and T is the total number of trade transactions. The theory develops by assuming certain of these factors to remain constant in the short run, or to change very slowly, and examines the cause and effect relationships between the remainder.

quasi-rent A term formerly used to describe all economic rents earned by factors of production other than land. Such differentiation is no longer made.

quota A limit imposed by on the quantity of a specified good that may be produced, purchased, exported or imported.

Rr

rate of interest The price of borrowed money. The difference between what is lent and what must be repaid, expressed as a percentage of the amount lent. For purposes of calculating rates for quotation, a loan period of one year is assumed.

rationing A system of allocating scarce goods by restricting the amount that a consumer can buy within a given period to a fixed quota which is based upon an estimate of available supplies.

real assets A firm's tangible productive resources such as land, buildings and machinery.

real gross national product A measure of the level of an economy's national product that has been adjusted to eliminate the effect of price changes. This enables comparisons of growth or decline between one year and another, free from the distorting effect of price level changes. It is calculated using the prices prevailing in a given base year.

real gross national product per capita The real gross national product divided by the number of people in the population. This enables true comparisons between one country and another, or over time within one country, by taking into account the size of the population over which the national product has to be distributed.

real income Earnings measured in terms of the goods and services they will buy. Changes in real income over time are calculated by adjusting the changes in money income by dividing them by an index number of retail prices.

real interest rate The effective gain in the value of money loaned or invested at a nominal rate of interest when allowance is made for inflation that has taken place during the period of the loan. The interest received will partially, totally or more than compensate for the loss in purchasing power of the sum invested. The real interest rate is the nominal interest rate minus the rate of inflation. If the inflation rate is higher than the interest rate, then the purchasing power of the sum invested will fall and the real interest rate will be negative.

real price A price of a commodity that has been adjusted to take account of the change in the general price level of all other commodities over a period of time. It measures to what extent the price of the commodity has changed relative to the general price level. If all prices have risen and the price of the commodity has risen by the same proportion, then its real price has not changed.

real wages Wages in terms of their purchasing power, that is, the amount of goods and services the money wages will buy. It is calculated by dividing the money wage by an index number of retail prices. If all prices have risen and wages have not risen proportionately, then real wages have fallen.

recession The downward turn following the peak of the trade cycle as demand falls off causing production and employment to decline. As unemployment grows, household incomes diminish. and cause demand to decline further. Firms start to get into difficulties as prices and profits fall. New investment now appears unprofitable and is reduced to a low level.

recovery Trade recovery.

redistribution of income The process of narrowing the range of inequality of incomes produced by the free-market processes. It is effected by the imposition of a progressive income tax structure alongside a scheme of social security payments.

reciprocal absolute advantage A situation where country A has an absolute advantage over country B in the production of one commodity, while B has an absolute advantage over A in another. Total production of both can be increased if each country specialises in the commodity in which it has absolute advantage and trades with the other.

regressive supply curve A graphical presentation of an abnormal market situation in which the fall in the price of a commodity beyond a certain point leads to an increase in the supply of that commodity, or conversely an increase in price leads to a fall in supply. The supply curve plotting these exceptional responses will, over the relative range, move in the opposite direction to its normal upward slope from left to right.

relative price A real price.

rent In the commercial sense of the term, payments made by tenants to landlords for the occupancy of land or buildings, or by hirers to suppliers for the lease of equipment. It is to be distinguished from the term *economic rent* as used in economic theory.

renewable resources Those such as timber, wildlife, fisheries, water supply, geothermal heat supplies, etc. whose stock is subject to replenishment by the processes of nature, providing there is no over-exploitation.

replacement investment The purchase of buildings, machinery, vehicles and other equipment in order to replace those which are worn out.

reserve currency A stable and easily convertible foreign currency which a government is willing to hold in its foreign exchange reserves and which it uses to finance a significant portion of its international trade.

reserve ratio The government-imposed minimum ratio that must be maintained by a bank between its total deposit liabilities and the cash reserves that it retains with the central bank.

retail Descriptive of the outlets which form the last stage in the chain of manufacture and distribution extending from the raw materials to the finished good. The retailers sell the final product direct to the individual for his own use.

retail prices index An index number designed to measure the change in the average retail price paid by households for the range of goods that they normally buy. It is often referred to as the cost of living index and is the base for calculating the inflation rate. It is calculated by choosing a an agreed selection of consumer goods, finding the current prices of those items, expressing these as percentages of their prices in an agreed base year, weighting each percentaged price by the average estimated amount that is bought by each household, and then calculating the average of these weighted percentaged prices.

returns to scale Rises in output caused by increasing the productive capacity of a firm by enlarging proportionately its plant, equipment and workforce. If output rises by a greater proportion than the increase in productive resources, returns to scale are said to be increasing. If output rises in the same proportion, they are said to be constant. If output rises by a lesser proportion, they are said to be decreasing.

revaluation The deliberate raising by the government of the value of its country's currency in terms of foreign currencies. Each unit of its currency exchanges for more dollars, francs, etc.

runaway inflation Hyperinflation.

Ss

saturation point A level beyond which the sale of a product or service is not expected to increase. It is expressed as a ratio, such as the number of units of the product per household or per hundred persons. Once this point has been reached, the growth of demand slows down to levels determined by population growth and replacement requirements.

saving That part of the income of individuals and firms that does not find its way back via spending into demand for goods and services. In the case of firms it is the undistributed profits which do not find their way back into personal incomes and hence into demand for goods and services.

savings, point of zero A level of disposable income at which it is all spent, hence no saving taking place. Above this point, out of each additional unit of income a percentage will be spent and the remainder will be saved. Below this point, dissaving will occur in the form of using up past savings or incurring debts.

scarcity A situation where there is less of something than people would like to have if it were free and available in unlimited quantities. Every nation's resources are insufficient to produce the quantities of goods and services that would be required to satisfy all of its people's wants in this sense. This gives rise to the need to allocate scarce productive resources among alternative uses.

seasonal unemployment Unemployment in those occupations where there is a demand for their services only at certain times of the year, usually because of weather conditions, holiday patterns or conventional concentrations of certain activities in certain months of the year.

secondary industry A manufacturing industry involved in the processing of raw materials into finished products.

services Benefits provided at a price to customers which involve the performance of some action by the seller that is advantageous, convenient, helpful or satisfying to the customer.

shift of supply curve Supply curve shift.

short run A time period in which, in order to respond to opportunities for increased output, a firm can increase its variable productive resources such as raw materials and manpower, but does not allow sufficient time for the firm to increase its fixed productive resources such as land, buildings and machinery. To do the latter may require one or two years.

short-run average fixed cost For any given level of a firm's output during a phase of expansion in which the fixed costs remain constant, the fixed cost per unit of output.

short-run average total cost For any given level of a firm's output during a phase of expansion in which the fixed costs remain constant, the total cost per unit of output.

short-run average variable cost For any given level of a firm's output during a phase of expansion in which the fixed costs remain constant, the variable cost per unit of output.

short-run marginal costs For any given level of a firm's output during a phase of expansion in which its fixed costs remain constant, the increase in total costs required to increase output by one unit.

shutdown price The selling price of a product which gains a firm just sufficient income to cover the variable cost of producing it. If the price falls below this level, the firm will cease production rather than produce at a loss.

slump A depression.

social benefits The total of the private financial benefits to a firm of its productive activity together with the external beneficial effects on the community of that activity. These may take the form of improved local employment opportunities, better roads and transport services, more shops and amenities, or the cleaning up of previously derelict sites.

social capital Assets such as roads, prisons, hospitals and schools which belong to the community as a whole rather than to private persons or firms.

social costs These include the private financial costs to a firm of its productive activity together with the external adverse effects on the community of that activity. These may take the form of pollution, noise, smell, congestion, loss of amenities, or environmental disfigurement.

social cost-benefit analysis Cost benefit analysis.

specialisation The concentration of workers on particular operations, or of firms or industries on particular products or stages of a productive process, in which they have a natural or an acquired advantage. The objectives are increased productivity and an improvement in quality. Specialisation also takes place on an international scale in the concentration of certain countries on certain products.

specific factors of production These are productive resources of a highly purpose-built kind such as intricate machinery that can be used only for the function for which it is designed and cannot satisfactorily be adjusted to serve alternative purposes.

speculative demand for money The holding of money in expectation of a fall in the price of securities or commodities so as to be ready to buy at the most advantageous moment.

stabilisation policy The fiscal and monetary measures which the government takes to reduce the scale of cyclical fluctuations in the level of economic activity of the country.

of production The sequence of process levels involved in the making of a good and bringing it to the customer, there being specialist industries operating at each level. One obtains the raw materials, another converts them into a basic product, another uses this to manufacture a semi-finished good, another incorporates this component into a finished good which is then be sold to a wholesaler to be resold to a retailer.

stagflation The co-existence of industrial stagnation or recession with continuing inflation.

standard of living The level of a person's material wellbeing. It is determined by the quantities, qualities and range of goods and services that he is able to buy, which in turn depends upon his disposable income and the availability and prices of the goods and services he requires.

stock appreciation Business profit arising from an increase in the value of goods held in stock. As this profit does not flow from the sale of goods, it must be excluded when calculating the domestic product.

stock levels At the start of each year a firm has a stock (or inventory) of unsold goods. At the end of the year it will have a stock of a different size. If the closing stock is greater than the opening stock, more was produced than was sold, resulting in stock piling. If the closing stock is less than the opening stock, less was produced than was sold, the running down of stock making up the difference.

stocks and flows A stock of a commodity refers to the amount that is available at a particular moment of time, that is the amount produced but unsold. The flow of a commodity is the amount that is sold during a specified period. If during the course of a year a commodity's production flow has exceeded its sales flow, then the stock level will have risen. The measure of the increase is found by the difference between the stock levels at the beginning and at the end of the year. To gain a true appreciation of what has taken place during the year, it is necessary to know the amount of the flow and of the change in stock level.

structural unemployment Long-lasting unemployment in a particular industry because the demand for its products has declined or because there has been an increase in the demand for imported goods at the expense of domestically produced goods. Because labour is not perfectly mobile to transfer from such a declining industry to an expanding one, unemployment tends to be heavily localised in the areas of the declining industry.

subsidies Payment by the government to a firm or an industry in order to prevent its decline, to avoid an increase in the prices of its products, or to enable its exports to compete more effectively on the international market.

subsistence The minimum level of provision of food, clothing and shelter necessary to ensure survival.

substitute goods Two commodities such as butter and margarine which are fairly good substitutes for one another because they perform a similar function or serve a similar taste. A rise in the price of one causes some degree of switchover to the substitute. The most important influence on the elasticity of demand for a commodity is whether it has close substitutes. The closer the available substitutes, the more elastic is likely to be its price elasticity of demand, providing the substitutes are within the same price range. If there are no close substitutes, demand is more likely to be inelastic.

substitute inputs For most forms of production, a firm can vary in the long run the proportions of its productive resources, employing more of one and less of another. A certain minimum amount of each is required, but above that it may be possible to substitute machines for manpower, or taller buildings for extra land space, etc.

substitution effect of changes in price The adjustment in the composition of a consumer's spending resulting solely from a change in relative prices. In the case of close substitutes, the one that has become relatively cheaper tends to be substituted for the other, the extent of the changeover depending on the closeness of the substitutes.

...nal profit The excess of actual profit over ...al profit. It is the income that rewards the owner's ...terprise in setting up the firm and taking the business risks. If entry into a particular business activity is perfectly free, then in the long run supernormal profits will reduce to zero. This is due to the competition of new entrepreneurs attracted to the market by the prospect of higher incomes than they are currently earning. Thus supernormal profits are either a short-run disequilibrium phenomenon or the result of barriers to entry.

supply The quantity of a good or service that suppliers will offer for sale during a given period in response to a particular price.

supply and demand, laws of A set of observations regarding the usual interrelated behaviour of market supply, demand and price. (1) If, at the prevailing price, demand exceeds supply, the price tends to rise, and conversely when supply exceeds demand. (2) A rise in price tends to contract demand and expand supply, and conversely with a fall in price. (3) Price tends to move to an equilibrium level at which demand is equal to the supply. (4) The greater the increase or fall in price, the greater the expansion or contraction of supply. (5) For any given price rise or fall, the expansion or contraction in the quantity supplied will be greater the longer the time the market is allowed to adjust.

supply curve The curve joining the points on a graph which plot the associated quantities and prices listed in a supply schedule. Quantities are measured on the horizontal axis and prices on the vertical axis. Since usually a higher price causes more to be supplied, the typical supply curve slopes upwards from left to right.

supply curve shift A graphical method of showing a change in the overall state of supply. This takes place when there is a change in the quantity of a product that suppliers are willing to bring to the market at each and every price. A new supply curve showing this changed situation must be drawn to the left or to the right of the original. An increase in quantity supplied at each price implies that the new supply curve appears (or shifts) to the right of the original. A reduced supply is shown as a new supply curve to the left of the original.

supply lag   The delay between the date of the decision to change the quantity supplied of a product and the date that the new level of supply appears on the market. Output currently coming onto the market is the result of production decisions taken in the past.

supply of labour   Labour supply.

supply of land   Considered as a country's total area in which production can take place, the supply of land is virtually fixed. No increase in rent can call forth any extra land. From the viewpoint of the use of the land, there are identifiable markets for land suitable for building, forestry, farming, recreation, etc. The total supply of land for any of these purposes can be varied only at the cost of changing from one land use to another.

supply schedule   A table showing for each of a series of levels of output per day, week, month, etc. the price per unit of output at which a firm would expect to sell the whole of that output. Alternatively, a table showing for each of a series of prices per unit of output, the output that a firm would expect to sell at that price.

supply side theory   A theory that proposes that the most effective method of increasing the national output and the level of employment is through the removal of tax disincentives. If personal taxes are reduced, people work harder so that there is a significant rise in output. If profit taxes are reduced, firms are encouraged to invest more, and this also leads to improved output. The resulting rise in national output causes the level of saving to rise. This reduces the interest rate which in its turn encourages further investment.

surplus   The amount of a commodity left unsold on the hands of the sellers because the market price is higher than the equilibrium price.

tariff, import Import tariff.

tax Money which an individual, a business or an organisation is required to pay to the government as a contribution to the finance of public expenditure. A direct tax is one which is assessed on the payer's income, profit or wealth, such as income tax, corporation tax and capital gains tax. An indirect tax is one which is paid as part of the price when a product or service is purchased, such as value added tax and duties on petrol, alcohol and tobacco.

tax incidence Incidence of indirect taxation.

technological progress The continual application of the knowledge acquired from scientific advance to the design of industrial and commercial equipment and methods of production. This results in more output per worker and per unit of equipment.

technological unemployment The displacement of workers because technological progress has introduced new labour-saving production techniques. Because labour is not perfectly mobile, there will be unemployment among those diplaced workers who have not managed to transfer to other industries or to retrain in the new occupational skills involved in the jobs created by the new technology.

technology A body of information, techniques, skills and experience, developed for the production and use of goods and services.

terms of trade The average price of a country's exports divided by the average price of the country's imports. In practice, the ratio of a country's price index of exports to its price index of imports. A rise (improvement) in this ratio

trade cycle

means that the income derived from a given quantity of exports will purchase a larger quantity of imports.

tight money policy The imposition of restrictions on the creation of credit, coupled with the maintainance of high rates of interest, in order to limit the level of borrowing for consumer spending. This may be an anti-inflationery measure and/or one designed to decrease the purchase of imports and so reduce an adverse balance of payments.

total cost The overall cost to a firm of producing a particular level of output. This consists of the firm's fixed costs plus the variable costs incurred in producing that output.

total revenue The income a firm receives from selling a particular quantity of its product. It is calculated by mutiplying the price the firm receives per unit of its product by the number of units sold.

total utility A term which summarises the total benefit in the form of satisfaction, convenience, help or advantage gained from the use of a number of units of some good or service. This is in distinction to marginal utility, which is the change in benefit resulting from having one unit more or less.

trade The exchange of commodities between individuals, firms or countries, rarely by direct barter and usually through the medium of money by purchase payments and sales receipts.

trade barrier Government limitations on the free international exchange of merchandise. They may take the form of tariffs, quotas, import licences, foreign currency controls or stringent regulations relating to health or safety standards.

trade cycle The uneven pattern experienced by most countries in the rate of their economic growth. It takes the form of alternating periods of years in which there is a contraction followed by an expansion in the level of their commercial and industrial activity.

trade recovery The expansionary phase of the trade cycle typified by a rise in employment, increased consumer spending, improved expectations encouraged by rises in production, sales and profits, optimism leading to commitment on investments that once seemed risky, the replacement of worn-out machinery, the expansion of production being facilitated by the availability of re-employable unused industrial capacity and unemployed workers.

transaction demand for money Money held by households and firms so as to be in a position to meet their day-to-day spending requirements.

transfer earnings The minimum amount that must be paid to any unit of a factor of production in order to to hold it in its present employment and prevent it from transferring to another use. Hence it is equal to the amount that the factor could earn in its best-paid alternative use.

transfer payments Payments made by public authorities to individuals for which no productive service is provided in return by the recipient. Examples are occupational pensions, student grants, government social security benefits and interest on money lent to the government.

transformation curve A curve which shows how good X can be transformed into good Y by reducing the output of X and transferring the resources thus saved into production of Y. It is drawn on the assumption that resources in the economy are fixed in total, and so shows the alternative combinations of X and Y that are technically feasible.

Uu

underpopulation   The situation of a country which has too few people to give rise to a workforce of sufficient size to take full advantage of the potential output of which the country's productive resources are capable. The contribution of additional workers would cause output to grow at a greater rate than the rate of increase of population, therefore output per person would rise.

undistributed profits   The part of after-tax profits that are kept in a firm and not paid out to its shareholders.

unearned income   Income derived from the ownership of assets such as the rent from leasing land, buildings or equipment, from interest on money loaned, or from dividends on shares.

unplanned economic system   A free market economy.

unemployment   A condition of involuntary idleness which exists when persons are capable of, available for, and seeking work as an employee, but cannot get a job.

unemployment rate   A measure of the extent of unemployment of the civilian labour force at any particular time. It is calculated by expressing the number of persons capable of working and willing to work but unable to find suitable employment, as a percentage of the total given by adding the number of such persons to the number in employment.

unfavourable balance of trade   An adverse balance of trade.

unit elasticity of demand   A market situation where a slight rise or fall in price of a good or service produces an exactly proportionate change in the amount demanded.

Accordingly there is no change in total expenditure on the good or service.

utility The satisfaction, advantage, help or convenience derived from consuming or using some quantity of a good or service. It is thus essentially a psychological concept which is incapable of measurement in absolute units. Utility does not depend upon any intrinsic value of the commodity, but upon the consumer's own subjective estimate of the need-fulfilment that it will yield him at a particular moment. Thus the same commodity will have different utilities for different people.

utility maximisation A basic assumption in economic theory that when a person is faced with having to make a choice between one combination of goods and services and another, he will always choose the alternative that will yield him the greatest need-fulfilment, that is, the maximum utility.

Vv

value added The revenue that a firm receives for the goods that it sells minus the cost of the raw materials bought from supplier firms in order to produce those goods. It thus measures the value which the firm has added to these bought-in materials in transforming them into saleable goods.

value judgement A statement of opinion that one situation is preferable to another on grounds of fairness, justice or morality.

value of service principle A pricing policy which may be adopted by a monopolist who enjoys the power to discriminate between markets. Within the total market a number of sub-markets are identified according to the differences in the value that customers place upon the service. The maximum gain is obtained from each sub-market by charging its customers the highest price that it is felt that they would be willing to pay.

variable costs Costs that change directly as the level of output changes, rising as more is produced and falling as less is produced. These include the costs of materials and power, and of labour that is employed as needed.

variable proportions, law of Diminishing marginal returns.

velocity of circulation The ratio between the value of a country's national product and the money supply available to finance all the transactions involved in purchasing that product. It may be regarded as the number of times in one year that the country's money supply has to circulate round the economy in order to buy the national product.

vertical integration The amalgamation into a single firm of firms previously engaged in successive stages in the production process of a commodity. This is done to achieve the greater security, stability and efficiency resulting from the centralised control and co-ordination of several stages of production.

vertical supply curve The graphical representation of a short-term market situation in which the total output of a commodity cannot be expanded in response to increasing demand. The supply 'curve' is a vertical line parallel to the price axis and thus indicating that at all prices the quantity coming to the market is the same.

visible balance The difference between the value of the goods imports and exports as recorded in one section of the current account of the balance of payments account.

visible trade International trade in tangible merchandise as distinct from *invisible* trade in intangible services.

volume of production The gross national product at factor cost.

voluntary exchange, principle of A person specialises in the production of good A and exchanges part of this output for good B, only if this procedure makes him better off. This requires that the quantity of good B that he obtains for one unit of good A must be greater than the quantity of good B that he could have produced if no specialisation had taken place. This advantage must be obtained also by the supplier of good B, otherwise no exchange would take place. The rate of exchange between the two goods must therefore satisfy both parties in this respect.

Ww

waiting An unavoidable feature of any plan to increase consumption through raising output by capital formation. The extra capital itself has to be produced before the increased production of consumer goods can take place. The accumulation of capital takes time and involves a sacrifice of present consumption for future consumption. The incentive to wait is the increased output that will eventually be obtained by the employment of more capital.

wasting assets Assets such as mineral deposits which are being used up in the process of production without possibility of renewal, and whose date of exhaustion determines the productive life of the venture.

wholesale trade That stage in the chain of production and distribution which consists of firms which buys goods in bulk from different manufacturers, hold stocks of these goods, and sell them in smaller quantities to retailers.

Zz

zero marginal utility The situation when a person's consumption of a good or service has reached the point where the acquiring of an extra unit of the good or service would give him no additional satisfaction.

zero opportunity cost The condition of long-term unemployed productive resources when they are eventually re-employed in production. Because there was no alternative activity to which they might have been allocated, their re-employment can be regarded as having taken place without any cost of reduced production elsewhere in the economy.

zero population growth A situation in which the population of a country remains constant.

zero savings, point of A level of disposable income at which it is all consumed. Above this point, out of each additional unit of income a percentage will be spent and the remainder will be saved. Below this point, dissaving will occur in the form of using up past savings or incurring debts.